500 RECIPES FOR EGG AND CHEESE DISHES

by Catherine Kirkpatrick

HAMLYN

Contents

Cover photograph by Paul Williams

Published by Hamlyn Publishing,
a division of The Hamlyn Publishing Group Limited,
Bridge House, London Road, Twickenham,
Middlesex, England

© Copyright Catherine Kirkpatrick 1966

All rights reserved. No part of this publication may
be reproduced, stored in a retrieval system, or
transmitted, in any form or by any means,
electronic, mechanical, photocopying, recording or
otherwise, without the permission of the
Copyrightholder and Hamlyn Publishing.

First published 1966
Revised edition 1971
Sixteenth impression 1985

ISBN 0 600 33049 4

Printed and bound in Great Britain by
R. J. Acford

Introduction

While I sympathise with the much quoted 'take a dozen eggs' of Mrs. Beeton, and with Ben Gunn in *Treasure Island* when he says 'Many's the night I've dreamed of cheese' – when it comes to 500 recipes for egg and cheese dishes I must confess that I am surprised that there is any need for such a book. Could anyone really need a book to tell them how to make an appetising meal out of eggs – as for cheese, it is surely the most perfect 'instant' food ever invented. But when one stops to think about it, is there any food more versatile than the egg? Any food having such a range of flavours and textures as cheese? Both are packed with essential nutrients, both can be prepared and cooked in the minimum of time, with no tedious preparation or waste.

If you still think that eggs are only for boiling and cheese for nibbling at the end of a meal, this book is not for you – unless you have, like me, suddenly realised that there are many good reasons for including dishes made from these two foods in our meal planning as often as possible. There is no end to the appetising ways in which these two foods can be combined with other ingredients to produce nourishing meals.

Before becoming involved in recipes, there is one important rule to be remembered whenever eggs or cheese are to be cooked – neither takes kindly to high temperatures. Both are rich in protein and high temperatures toughen protein – with very unappetising results.

Hints on cooking and storing

Always cook eggs slowly – with a slow to moderate heat

High temperatures and over-cooking cause curdling and 'watering' in dishes thickened with eggs, while soufflés and other dishes leavened with eggs will have a tough crust and become rubbery inside. There is no need to be ashamed that you 'can't even boil an egg' – a good cook never boils an egg. As with many other foods, when we say boil, in this context, we mean, bring to boiling point, reduce heat quickly and hold at simmering point.

Always cook cheese very gently and not more than necessary

Over-heating and over-cooking tend to make cheese tough and indigestible. When making a cheese sauce for example, add the cheese at the last minute and continue to cook the mixture only long enough to melt the cheese. Better still, if the cheese is finely grated, remove the pan from the heat and allow the heat of the sauce to melt it. Like egg dishes, most cheese dishes should be cooked at a slow or moderate temperature.

Choice of cheese is important

Cheddar is the cheese most widely used in cooking in this country, though crumbly Lancashire is the one to choose, especially for toasting. Of the foreign cheese, Parmesan is the most at home in the kitchen, as it has, in addition to its excellent flavour, the advantage of being very hard, so can be grated finely. Parmesan can also be bought ready grated and is suitable for all made up cheese dishes. But it is more expensive than Cheddar or Lancashire.

Storage of cheese

Cheese will keep, well wrapped in foil, cellophane, or in a polythene bag. Keep it in a cool place – the refrigerator or a cold larder. Do not wrap cheese in greaseproof paper as this tends to draw out the fat. If the cheese gets white bloom on it, this is easily scraped off and the cheese will be perfectly all right to eat.
Do remember that for the best flavour, cheese should be at room temperature for at least one hour before eating.

Storage of eggs

Eggs require cool storage in an atmosphere that is not too dry. Keep eggs broad end up and away from strongly flavoured food like some cheese and onions. The porous nature of the shell makes the contents particularly receptive to external odours.
Eggs kept in a refrigerator should be removed one hour before use and allowed to come to room temperature.

Tips for using up cheese

Grate cheese, several kinds can be mixed together.

Add a little freshly ground black pepper and some softened butter, using about 1 oz. to 8 oz. cheese.
Moisten with a little white wine and beat till creamy. Press into a basin and cover with melted butter. Keep in a cold place and use as a sandwich spread or on toast or crispbread.

Choice of eggs for cooking

The Romans believed that long eggs had better flavour than round eggs, just as many people today believe that brown eggs taste better than white, but when it comes to cooking, it is the size that is important. Eggs are graded according to their weight: Large, Standard, Medium and Small.
In cooking it is advisable to use standard eggs – unless the size is specified. In liquid capacity there are an average 12 standard eggs, shelled, to the pint. 12 small eggs yield only $\frac{3}{4}$ pint, hence the importance in a balanced recipe, a large cake for example, to use eggs of the correct size.
When choosing cheese for the end of a meal remember that each cheese has an individual taste. Here is a guide:
For men, select a strong cheese: Cheddar for its nutty flavour, Stilton, rich and mellow, or Double Gloucester, a pungent smooth textured cheese or a matured Lancashire.
Many children prefer a cheese to sweet things and there's nothing better for an in-between-meals nibble. Give them Wensleydale, a creamy cheese with a honeyed after-taste, or Caerphilly with its gentle, milk flavour.
To suit feminine taste, choose a cheese of medium flavour such as Cheshire, mellow with a salty tang, Leicester, a real dessert cheese known by its rich russet colour, or Derby, a very close textured cheese.

Some Useful Facts and Figures

Notes on metrication

In case you wish to convert quantities into metric measures, the following tables give a comparison.

Solid measures

Ounces	Approx. grams to nearest whole figure	Recommended conversion to nearest unit of 25
1	28	25
2	57	50
3	85	75
4	113	100
5	142	150
6	170	175
7	198	200
8	227	225
9	255	250
10	283	275
11	312	300
12	340	350
13	368	375
14	396	400
15	425	425
16 (1 lb)	454	450
17	482	475
18	510	500
19	539	550
20 (1$\frac{1}{4}$ lb)	567	575

Note: When converting quantities over 20 oz first add the appropriate figures in the centre column, then adjust to the nearest unit of 25. As a general guide, 1 kg (1000 g) equals 2·2 lb or about 2 lb 3 oz. This method of conversion gives good results in nearly all cases, although in certain pastry and cake recipes a more accurate conversion is necessary to produce a balanced recipe.

Liquid measures

Imperial	Approx. millilitres to nearest whole figure	Recommended millilitres
$\frac{1}{4}$ pint	142	150
$\frac{1}{2}$ pint	283	300
$\frac{3}{4}$ pint	425	450
1 pint	567	600
1$\frac{1}{2}$ pints	851	900
1$\frac{3}{4}$ pints	992	1000 (1 litre)

Oven temperatures

The table below gives recommended equivalents.

	°C	°F	Gas Mark
Very cool	110	225	$\frac{1}{4}$
	120	250	$\frac{1}{2}$
Cool	140	275	1
	150	300	2
Moderate	160	325	3
	180	350	4
Moderately hot	190	375	5
	200	400	6
Hot	220	425	7
	230	450	8
Very hot	240	475	9

Notes for American and Australian users

In America the 8-oz measuring cup is used. In Australia metric measures are now used in conjunction with the standard 250-ml measuring cup. The Imperial pint, used in Britain and Australia, is 20 fl oz, while the American pint is 16 fl oz. It is important to remember that the Australian tablespoon differs from both the British and American tablespoons. The British standard tablespoon, which has been used throughout this book, holds 17·7 ml, the American 14·2 ml, and the Australian 20 ml. A teaspoon holds approximately 5 ml in all three countries.

Oven temperatures

The table below gives recommended equivalents.

Description	°C	°F	Gas Mark
VERY COOL	110	225	$\frac{1}{4}$
	120	250	$\frac{1}{2}$
COOL	140	275	1
	150	300	2
MODERATE	160	325	3
	180	350	4
MODERATELY HOT	190	375	5
	200	400	6
HOT	220	425	7
	230	450	8
VERY HOT	240	475	9

Breakfast dishes

No food is as versatile as the egg. For breakfast, lunch or supper there are dozens of ways of serving them but for breakfast they are particularly suitable, being light and nutritious, easy and quick to prepare. Eggs contain protein, fat, vitamins A, B and D, iron, phosphorus and calcium, all necessary for growth and good health.

To boil
The exact time is very much a matter of personal taste. There are three methods and the times given should be taken as an average.
1 Immerse eggs in boiling water and allow $3\frac{1}{2}$ minutes for large and standard eggs, and 3 minutes for small ones.
2 Put eggs into cold water, bring to the boil; for large eggs simmer for 3 minutes, for standard $2\frac{3}{4}$ minutes, and for small ones $2\frac{1}{2}$ minutes.
3 Immerse eggs in boiling water, cover pan and draw it away from the heat. For large and standard eggs leave for 8–9 minutes and for small ones 7–8 minutes.

To hard-boil
Put eggs into cold water and bring to boiling point, then reduce heat and simmer only. For large eggs allow 12 minutes, for standard size 11 minutes and for small eggs 10 minutes.
As soon as they are cooked, plunge eggs into cold running water and cool rapidly. This will prevent a dark ring forming between the yolk and white of the egg.

To poach
Use a shallow pan and be sure there is enough water to cover eggs completely.
Bring water to boiling point, then reduce heat until water is just simmering. Break an egg into a cup and slip it carefully into the water.
If the water is stirred before adding the egg, it will keep a good round shape.
Simmer for 3–5 minutes depending on how firm you wish the egg to be.
Do not let the water boil or the egg will be tough. When it is ready, remove egg with a perforated spoon and serve on hot buttered toast.

To fry
Heat about 2 tablespoons fat in a frying pan. Break the eggs and slip them gently into the pan. Reduce heat and cook slowly for 3–4 minutes, basting well with the fat.
If you prefer the eggs cooked on both sides, turn over carefully with a slice. Basting is not necessary.

To scramble
For 2 eggs allow 2 tablespoons milk or cream and $\frac{1}{2}$ oz. butter. *continued*

5

Beat eggs lightly, add milk and seasoning.
Heat butter, pour in the egg mixture and constantly stir over low heat until egg thickens. Remove at once from heat and serve.

Additional flavouring for scrambled eggs

For every 2 eggs, add one of the following:
(*a*) 1 tablespoon diced sautéed **bread cubes** or cooked potato with ½ teaspoon chopped **chives**.
(*b*) 1 cooked **chicken liver**, finely chopped and fried with chopped **bacon**.
(*c*) 2 tablespoons chopped cooked **ham, tongue or chicken**.
(*d*) 2 tablespoons flaked, cooked **fish**.
(*e*) 2 oz. chopped cooked **mushrooms**.
(*f*) 1 tablespoon chopped **parsley and chives**.
(*g*) 1½ oz. grated **cheese**.
(*h*) 2–3 slices **liver sausage,** chopped.
(*i*) 2 sliced cooked **sausages or frankfurters**.

Bacon with apple

cooking time: about 10 minutes

you will need for 4 servings:

2 eggs	1½ oz. butter
4 tablespoons milk	4 rashers bacon
salt, pepper	4 apple rings
4 slices bread	

1 Beat eggs with milk, add seasoning and put into a shallow dish.
2 Remove crusts from bread and soak slices in egg until well moistened.
3 Heat butter, and fry bread till golden brown on both sides.
4 Remove and keep hot.
5 Fry bacon and apple rings, then arrange a rasher of bacon and an apple ring on each piece of bread. Serve piping hot.

Bacon and kidney scramble

cooking time: about 15 minutes

you will need for 4 servings:

2 kidneys	3 eggs
1½ oz. butter	1 tablespoon top of the
4 rashers streaky bacon	milk
salt, pepper	4 rounds buttered toast
pinch mixed herbs	

1 Skin kidneys, remove cores and slice thinly.
2 Heat butter, add kidneys and chopped bacon and fry till kidney is tender.
3 Add seasoning and herbs.
4 Beat eggs with milk, pour over kidneys and stir over gentle heat till eggs are lightly set.
5 Serve on toast.

Bacon scramble

cooking time: 10–12 minutes

you will need for 4 servings:

4 rashers bacon	3 eggs
3 tablespoons cooked rice	salt, pepper
3 tablespoons milk	4 rounds buttered toast

1 Chop bacon and fry till crisp.
2 Add rice and milk and stir for a few minutes over the heat.
3 Beat eggs, season and add to rice mixture.
4 Stir over gentle heat until eggs are lightly set.
5 Serve on toast.

Baked eggs

cooking time: 10 minutes

you will need for 1 serving:

½ oz. butter	salt, pepper
1 egg	

1 Put butter in the bottom of a small ovenproof dish. Place dish on a baking tray.
2 Place in a moderate oven (350°F. – Gas Mark 4) until the butter has melted.
3 Break egg into the dish, season lightly with salt and pepper.
4 Return to oven and bake until egg is set (5–8 minutes). Serve at once, accompanied by toast or with cooked vegetables or salad.

Variation

With **cheese** – sprinkle egg with 1 teaspoon finely grated cheese and cook under grill until yolk is just set, about 5 minutes.

Baked egg with potato

cooking time: 5 minutes

you will need for 1 serving:

butter	1 egg
2–3 tablespoons creamed	seasoning
potato	grated cheese

1 Grease a small ovenproof dish and line with potato.
2 Break egg into the centre, season lightly with salt and pepper. Sprinkle with cheese.
3 Bake in a moderate oven (350°F. – Gas Mark 4) until set, about 6 minutes.

Baked Swiss egg

cooking time: 15–20 minutes

you will need for 1 serving

butter	1 egg
cheese	seasoning

1 Grease a small ovenproof dish and line with thin slices cheese, preferably Gruyère.

2 Break egg over cheese. Season lightly.

3 Dot with butter, bake in a moderate oven (350°F. – Gas Mark 4) 15–20 minutes.

4 Serve at once in the ovenproof dish. If liked, garnish with parsley.

Cheese and potato cakes

cooking time: 5–7 minutes

you will need for 4 servings:

8 oz. potatoes	salt, pepper
1 oz. self-raising flour	fat for frying
4 oz. grated cheese	

1 Peel potatoes and grate finely.

2 Add flour, cheese and seasoning and mix well.

3 Heat fat and fry mixture in spoonfuls, turning over.

4 Drain and serve with fried bacon or tomatoes.

Cheese scramble

cooking time: 5–6 minutes

you will need for 4 servings:

¼ oz. butter	4 rounds buttered toast
4 oz. cream cheese	chopped parsley or
4 eggs	paprika
salt, Cayenne pepper	

1 Melt butter, add cheese and beaten eggs.

2 Season, then stir over very gentle heat until eggs are set.

3 Pile on toast and sprinkle with a little parsley or paprika.

Egg and sausage cakes

cooking time: 15 minutes

you will need for 4 servings:

8 oz. sausage meat	flour
¼ small apple, peeled and	fat for frying
finely chopped	4 eggs

1 Mix sausage meat with apple, divide into 4 portions and shape each into a round flat cake.

2 Coat with flour and fry till cooked and brown on both sides. Remove from pan and keep hot.

3 Fry eggs and serve one on each sausage cake. Serve with grilled tomatoes.

Fried eggs with black butter

cooking time: 4–5 minutes

you will need for each serving:

1 egg	salt, pepper
2 tablespoons butter	1 teaspoon vinegar
1 round buttered toast	
or fried bread	

1 Fry egg in 1 tablespoon butter and put on toast or fried bread.

2 Add remaining butter to pan and allow it to brown.

3 Add salt, pepper and vinegar.

4 Make very hot and pour over the egg. Serve immediately.

Fried eggs with ham

cooking time: 4–5 minutes

you will need for each serving:

2 oz. cooked ham	1 egg
butter	1 round buttered toast
little chopped parsley	or fried bread

1 Chop ham and heat with a little butter and parsley.

2 Fry egg in butter.

3 Serve on the bread and surround with ham.

Haddock scramble

cooking time: 3–4 minutes

you will need for 4 servings:

4 eggs	1½ oz. butter
1 tablespoon water	4 rounds buttered toast
salt, pepper, little made	chopped parsley or
mustard	tarragon
6 oz. cooked smoked]	
haddock	

1 Beat eggs lightly with water and seasoning.

2 Flake fish finely and mix with egg.

3 Heat butter, add egg and fish mixture and stir over gentle heat, until mixture is creamy.

4 Serve on hot toast and sprinkle with parsley or tarragon.

Kippered eggs

cooking time: 5–6 minutes

you will need for 4 servings:

8 oz. cooked kipper	1 oz. butter
4 eggs	4 rounds buttered toast
salt, pepper	chopped parsley
1 tablespoon water	

1 Remove any bones from the fish and flake finely.

2 Beat eggs and add salt sparingly, pepper and water.

3 Mix fish and beaten eggs together.

4 Heat butter, add mixture and stir over gentle heat until eggs are lightly set.

5 Pile on to toast and sprinkle with parsley.

Poached eggs on spinach

cooking time: 10 minutes

you will need for 2 servings:

1 small packet frozen	2 eggs
creamed spinach	¼ pint cheese sauce (see
salt, pepper	page 91)
pinch nutmeg	little grated Parmesan
1 tablespoon cream	cheese

1 Prepare spinach according to the directions on the

packet. Drain well, add seasoning, nutmeg and cream and put into a small fireproof dish. Keep hot.

2 Poach eggs (see page 5) and arrange on the spinach.
3 Cover with sauce, sprinkle with cheese and brown under the grill.

Scrambled eggs duxelle

cooking time: 3–4 minutes

you will need for 4 servings:

6 eggs	1 oz. cooked mushrooms
2 oz. butter	4 rounds buttered toast
salt, pepper	chopped parsley, optional
2 oz. cooked ham	

1 Beat eggs lightly.

2 Melt butter, add eggs and seasoning.
3 Cook over gentle heat until eggs begin to thicken, then add finely chopped ham and mushrooms.
4 When just firm and creamy, pile on to rounds of toast and serve.
5 If liked, sprinkle with chopped parsley.

Fish

Fish au gratin

cooking time: 15–20 minutes

you will need for 4 servings:

12 oz. cooked white fish	1 egg, separated
1 4-oz. can shrimps	2 tablespoons grated
salt, pepper	cheese
lemon juice	½ oz. butter
milk or fish stock	chopped parsley, optional
¼ pint cheese sauce (see page 91)	

1 Skin and bone, then flake fish.
2 Reserve a few shrimps for garnish, mix the rest with fish.
3 Add seasoning, lemon juice to taste and, if necessary, moisten fish with a little milk or fish stock. Put into a buttered fireproof dish.
4 Make the sauce, cool a little, then stir in egg yolk and fold in stiffly beaten egg white.
5 Pour over fish. Sprinkle with cheese and dot with butter.
6 Bake for about 15 minutes in a moderate oven (350°F. – Gas Mark 4).
7 Serve hot, garnished with reserved shrimps and a little finely chopped parsley.

Fish cream

cooking time: about 40 minutes

you will need for 4 servings:

4 oz. whiting or fresh haddock	salt, pepper
	lemon juice
½ oz. butter	1 dessertspoon grated
1 egg, separated	cheese
1 tablespoon milk	¼ pint cream
½ oz. fresh white bread- crumbs	1–2 drops cochineal

1 Skin and bone fish and shred finely.

2 Melt butter, add egg yolk beaten with milk and breadcrumbs. Cook till mixture is thick but do not allow to boil.
3 Add fish. Rub all through a sieve.
4 Add seasoning, lemon juice to taste, cheese and cream.
5 Beat egg white stiffly and fold in.
6 Add 1–2 drops cochineal to improve the colour.
7 Turn into a small buttered basin, cover with buttered paper and steam very gently for 40 minutes.
8 Turn out carefully and serve with white or cheese sauce (see page 91).

Fish pudding

cooking time: 1½ hours

you will need for 4 servings:

1 lb. white fish or 8 oz. white fish and 8 oz. smoked haddock	¼ pint milk or stock made from fish bones
4 oz. shredded suet	2 eggs
2 oz. breadcrumbs	salt, pepper
1 teaspoon finely chopped parsley	2 tomatoes

1 Remove the skin and bones from the fish. Pound it well or chop finely and rub it through a sieve or coarse mincer.
2 When smooth, work in the suet.
3 Add all the other ingredients except the tomatoes.
4 Slice the tomatoes and use to cover the bottom of a greased basin.
5 Press the fish mixture into the basin, cover with greased paper and steam.
6 Serve with melted butter sauce or a plain white sauce.

Creamed prawns

cooking time: 10 minutes

you will need for 4 servings:

8 oz. prawns	salt and pepper to taste
2 oz. butter	4 slices hot toast,
2 teaspoons lemon juice	unbuttered
4 tablespoons soured	chopped parsley or
cream	nutmeg
yolks of 2 eggs	

1 Put prawns and butter in a pan, and heat gently for 5 minutes, taking care that the butter does not brown.
2 Stir in lemon juice, soured cream and egg yolks.
3 Cook over a low heat, stirring all the time, until the sauce thickens. Do not allow the sauce to boil.
4 Season to taste with salt and pepper.
5 Pile mixture on toast. Sprinkle with chopped parsley or grated nutmeg.

Tuna grill

cooking time: 20 minutes

you will need for 4 servings:

1 7–oz. can tuna fish	**topping:**
¾ pint white sauce (see	4 slices bread, crusts
page 91)	removed
8 oz. cooked mixed	butter
vegetables	1–2 oz. grated cheese
seasoning	
lemon juice	

1 Drain and flake the tuna, add to the sauce with the vegetables.
2 Season to taste, add lemon juice and heat thoroughly. Turn into an ovenproof dish.
3 Spread bread with butter and cut each slice into 4 triangles.
4 Arrange round the edge of the dish, sprinkle with cheese and brown under a medium grill.

Fish pie

cooking time: 30 minutes

you will need for 4 servings:

1 lb. cooked white fish	¼ pint cheese sauce (see
salt, pepper	page 91)
1 tablespoon chopped	1 lb. mashed potatoes
capers	2 oz. butter
1 dessertspoon anchovy	3–4 tablespoons milk
essence	3 oz. grated cheese
2 hard-boiled eggs	1–2 tomatoes

1 Skin and bone fish, then flake it.
2 Add seasoning, capers and anchovy essence.
3 Put into buttered fireproof dish; add sliced eggs.
4 Cover with cheese sauce.
5 Beat potatoes with 1 oz. butter and a little milk; adjust seasoning if necessary, then put on top of the sauce.
6 Sprinkle with cheese and dot with remaining butter.

7 Peel and slice tomatoes and arrange round the edge of the dish.
8 Bake in a moderately hot oven (400°F. – Gas Mark 6) for 30 minutes.

Fish custard

cooking time: 20–25 minutes

you will need for 2 servings:

2 fillets sole	½ pint milk
1 egg	salt, pepper

1 Skin the fillets and roll up with the skinned side inside. Place in a buttered basin.
2 Beat egg, add milk and seasoning and pour over fish.
3 Cover with buttered paper and stand the basin in a pan of boiling water.
4 Reduce heat at once, cover and simmer gently for about 20–25 minutes.
5 Remove paper and serve immediately.

Savoury fish custard

cooking time: about 30 minutes

you will need for 4 servings:

8 oz. cooked smoked	½ pint milk
haddock	salt, pepper
3 eggs	1 teaspoon chopped
3 level teaspoons	parsley or a pinch
cornflour	mixed herbs

1 Flake the fish very finely and put it into a greased fireproof dish.
2 Mix the eggs smoothly with the cornflour, add the milk gradually and beat all well together.
3 Add seasoning and parsley and pour over the fish.
4 Bake in a moderate oven (375°F. – Gas Mark 5).

Cheese and salmon bake

cooking time: 45 minutes

you will need for 4 servings:

6 oz. long grain rice	salt, pepper
¾ pint water	1 heaped tablespoon
¼ teaspoon salt	breadcrumbs
3 oz. grated cheese	1 oz. butter
¾ pint thick white sauce	1 lemon
1 7½-oz. can salmon	

1 Put rice, water and salt into a saucepan. Bring to the boil, stir once. Cover tightly and simmer for 15 minutes.
2 Add the cheese to the white sauce, plus the liquid from the salmon. Season to taste.
3 Flake the salmon with a fork.
4 Grease the inside of an ovenproof dish. Fill dish with alternate layers of rice, salmon and sauce, finishing with a layer of rice.
5 Sprinkle with breadcrumbs and dot with butter.

continued

6 Bake in a moderate oven (350°F. – Gas Mark 4) for 30 minutes. Serve hot, garnished with slices of lemon.

Variation

Cheese, egg and salmon bake – to vary this dish, add 1 or 2 chopped hard-boiled eggs to the sauce, plus one heaped tablespoon chopped parsley.

Hake au gratin

cooking time: 15–20 minutes

you will need for 4 servings:

8 oz. cooked hake	2 oz. grated cheese
1 4-oz. can shrimps	2 bananas
½ pint white sauce (see page 91)	lemon juice
	little butter
1 egg	

1 Flake the fish, removing all skin and bone.

2 Add the shrimps, reserving a few for garnish.

3 Make the white sauce, cool a little then add the yolk of egg and half the cheese.

4 Whisk the egg white stiffly and fold into the sauce.

5 Put fish into a fireproof dish and pour sauce over.

6 Sprinkle with the remaining cheese and dot with butter.

7 Bake in a moderate oven (350°F. – Gas Mark 4) for about 15 minutes.

8 Slice the bananas, brush with lemon juice and a little melted butter.

9 Arrange round the edge of the dish and return to the oven for a further 5 minutes.

Haddock savoury

cooking time: 10 minutes

you will need for 4 servings:

8 oz. cooked smoked haddock	2 oz. grated cheese
1 oz. butter	Cayenne pepper
1 egg	squeeze lemon juice
1–2 tablespoons milk	4 rounds buttered toast
	chopped parsley

1 Flake fish finely and put into a pan with the butter, beaten egg, milk and cheese.

2 Stir over gentle heat till mixture is quite hot and thick.

3 Add a pinch Cayenne and lemon juice.

4 Pile on hot toast and sprinkle with parsley.

Fish and cheese savoury

cooking time: about 30 minutes

you will need for 4 servings:

1 lb. smoked haddock	3 tomatoes
salt, pepper	little sugar
½ pint white sauce (see page 91)	2 slices bread
	4 oz. cheese
2 teaspoons capers	

1 Sprinkle the fish with salt and pepper and steam between two plates.

2 When cooked, flake into a bowl.

3 Add the capers to the white sauce.

4 Halve the tomatoes, sprinkle with salt, pepper and a little sugar. Grill until brown. Keep hot.

5 Toast the bread.

6 Add the fish to the sauce and heat gently.

7 Meanwhile, cut the cheese into slices and when the fish is heated through, pour it into an ovenproof dish and cover with the cheese.

8 Place under the grill until golden brown.

9 Serve with the tomatoes and toast.

Scalloped fish

cooking time: 25–30 minutes

you will need for 4 servings:

1 lb. cod or haddock fillet	1 tablespoon bread-crumbs
8 oz. spaghetti	little butter
2 rashers streaky bacon	chopped parsley or paprika
1–2 hard-boiled eggs	
1 pint cheese sauce (see page 91)	
1 tablespoon grated cheese	

1 Cook the fish, remove all skin and bone and flake finely.

2 Cook the spaghetti in boiling salted water.

3 Chop the bacon and fry till crisp.

4 Mix the fish and spaghetti together, add bacon and chopped hard-boiled eggs. Season as required and put all into a casserole.

5 Make the cheese sauce and pour over the contents of the casserole.

6 Mix the cheese and breadcrumbs together and sprinkle on top.

7 Dot with butter and bake in a moderate oven (350°F. – Gas Mark 4).

8 Garnish with parsley or paprika.

Fish puffs

cooking time: 5–10 minutes

you will need for 4 servings:

8 oz. cooked white fish	2 eggs
salt, pepper	1 oz. flour
lemon juice	fat, deep for frying
2 teaspoons anchovy essence	

1 Flake the fish very finely, removing all skin and bone.

2 Season very carefully and add lemon juice and anchovy essence.

3 Add the egg yolks and the flour and beat until the mixture is creamy.

4 Fold in the stiffly beaten egg whites.

5 Drop spoonfuls into hot fat and fry until crisp and well puffed.

6 Drain and serve.

Cheese and fish risotto

cooking time: 30 minutes

you will need for 4 servings:
8 oz. long grain rice	salt, pepper
1 pint water	2 oz. grated Parmesan
1 teaspoon salt	cheese
1 lb. ripe tomatoes	2 tablespoons chopped
1 onion, finely chopped	chives or parsley
1 oz. butter	
8 oz. smoked haddock, cooked	

1 Put rice, water and salt into a saucepan. Bring to the boil, stir once, cover tightly and simmer for 15 minutes.
2 Peel the tomatoes and chop roughly. Fry onion in butter for 5 minutes, add tomatoes.
3 Flake haddock, add to onion tomato mixture, and cook for 10 minutes. Season to taste with salt and pepper.
4 Turn rice out on to a warm serving dish. Pour tomato mixture over.
5 Sprinkle with grated cheese and chives or parsley.

Omelettes

The preparation and cooking of an omelette should only take a matter of minutes.
Recipes for more substantial omelettes will be found in the sections of Luncheon and Supper dishes and Snacks but a basic recipe follows.

Points to remember

1 A heavy pan should be used and it must not be too large – an omelette using up to 4 eggs requires a pan 6–7 inches in diameter.
2 Unsalted butter, margarine or oil is best used for frying.
3 A pan should be kept for omelettes and pancakes. The pan should not be washed. After use rub with soft paper, wipe with a clean cloth.

Basic omelette

cooking time: 1–1½ minutes

you will need for 1 serving:
2 eggs	salt, pepper
2 teaspoons water	½ oz. butter

1 Break eggs and beat with a fork until only lightly frothy. Add water and seasoning.
2 Heat butter in a small strong frying pan and, as soon as it is frothy, pour in egg mixture.
3 Leave for about 10 seconds when mixture will have set on the bottom, then stir with a fork and move the pan around so that the mixture which is still liquid comes in contact with the hot pan.
4 Loosen edges, tilt pan away from you and, with a palette knife, fold omelette over. Serve at once.

Variation

With herbs and meat – chopped parsley, mixed herbs, a little finely chopped ham or tongue can be mixed with the eggs before frying.

Asparagus omelette

cooking time: 5–6 minutes

you will need for 3 servings:
3–4 heads cooked fresh or canned asparagus	1 teaspoon cornflour
2 eggs	1 dessertspoon milk
salt, pepper	butter for frying

1 Heat asparagus. Beat eggs, add seasoning and cornflour, mixed smoothly with the milk.
2 Heat butter till frothy, pour in egg mixture.
3 Cook omelette in the usual way. Put a little of the asparagus in the centre. Fold over and serve remaining asparagus separately.

Bacon omelette

cooking time: 3–4 minutes

you will need for 1 serving:
1–2 rashers bacon	salt, pepper
2 eggs	butter for frying
2 teaspoons water	

1 Remove rind and cut the bacon into small pieces. Fry until crisp.
2 Beat eggs with water, add bacon and season carefully.
3 Heat butter till frothy, pour in egg and bacon mixture and cook omelette in the usual way.

Baked omelette

cooking time: about 40 minutes

you will need for 3 servings:
6 rashers streaky bacon	salt, pepper
½ small onion, minced or finely chopped	¼ pint milk
6 eggs	4 oz. grated cheese
	chopped parsley

1 Halve bacon rashers and fry lightly. *continued*

11

2 Remove from pan, add onion and fry in bacon fat till soft and lightly browned.

3 Put onion into a buttered fireproof dish.

4 Beat eggs, add seasoning and milk and pour into dish.

5 Sprinkle with cheese and arrange bacon on top.

6 Bake in a moderate oven (350° F. – Gas Mark 4) till just firm on top. Sprinkle with parsley before serving.

Bacon and potato omelette

cooking time: 8–10 minutes

you will need for 2 servings:

for the filling:	for the omelette:
4 rashers streaky bacon	3 eggs
2–3 cooked potatoes	3 teaspoons water
2 tablespoons bacon fat	salt, pepper
or butter	½ oz. butter
1 tablespoon chopped	
parsley	
salt, pepper	

1 Remove rind from bacon and cut into strips. Dice potatoes.

2 Heat fat and fry bacon and potatoes till well browned. Add parsley and seasoning and keep hot.

3 Make omelette in the usual way. Place filling in the centre, fold over and turn on to a hot dish.

Baked ham omelette

cooking time: about 10 minutes

you will need for 2 servings:

2 eggs	1 teaspoon chopped
salt, pepper	parsley
2 tablespoons milk	1 oz. cooked ham, finely
	chopped

1 Separate eggs, beat yolks till creamy, add seasoning, milk, parsley and ham.

2 Beat egg whites stiffly and fold into the mixture.

3 Put into a buttered shallow fireproof dish and bake about 10 minutes in a moderate oven (350°F. – Gas Mark 4). Serve at once.

Cheese soufflé omelette

cooking time: 7–8 minutes

you will need for 2 servings:

	for the filling:
½ oz. cornflour	1 oz. grated cheese
¼ pint milk	½ oz. butter
salt, pepper	1 tablespoon milk
2 eggs, separated	salt, pepper
butter for frying	little made mustard

1 Mix cornflour smoothly with milk. Stir till boiling and boil for 1 minute. Add seasoning and, when cooked a little, stir egg yolks in.

2 Beat egg whites stiffly and fold into mixture.

3 Heat some butter in an omelette pan till frothy. Pour egg mixture in and cook till set and lightly browned underneath.

4 Put under grill to brown the top.

5 Meanwhile melt cheese with butter and milk. Add seasoning.

6 Pour cheese mixture in the centre of the omelette, fold over and serve at once.

Cheese omelette with croûtons

cooking time: 5–6 minutes

you will need for 2 servings:

1 slice bread	2 tablespoons water
butter	2 tablespoons grated
3 eggs	cheese
salt, pepper	

1 Cut crusts from bread and dice it. Fry in butter till crisp and golden brown, then remove from pan and keep hot.

2 Beat eggs with seasoning and water.

3 Add a little more butter to the pan if necessary and, when it is hot, pour in eggs and cook the omelette in the usual way (see page 11).

4 When it is just set underneath, add croûtons and cheese.

5 Fold omelette over and slide on to a hot dish.

Curry omelette

cooking time: 5–6 minutes

you will need for 2 servings:

3 eggs	1 tablespoon cooked rice,
½ teaspoon curry powder	heated in a little butter
2 tablespoons water	butter for frying
salt	

1 Beat eggs with the curry powder, water and salt.

2 Cook omelette in the usual way (see page 11), fill with rice and fold over.

Serve with tomato sauce (see page 91).

Devilled ham omelette

cooking time: 3–4 minutes

you will need for 2 servings:

3 eggs	2 tablespoons thin cream
¼ teaspoon dry mustard	2 oz. cooked ham, finely
pinch curry powder	chopped
salt, Cayenne pepper	½ oz. butter
2 tablespoons water	

1 Beat eggs lightly, add seasoning, water, cream and ham.

2 Heat butter in an omelette pan, pour in egg mixture

and leave for a few seconds, then stir with a fork as it begins to set, loosen the omelette from the sides of the pan.

3 When just set underneath, put under a grill to brown top. Fold over and serve at once.

Fish omelette

cooking time: 3–4 minutes

you will need for 2 servings:

2 eggs	¼ teaspoon chopped
salt, pepper	capers
2 tablespoons milk	butter for frying
4 oz. flaked cooked fish	

1 Beat eggs, add seasoning and other ingredients.
2 Heat butter in an omelette pan and, when frothy, pour in the egg and fish mixture.
3 Cook omelette in the usual way (see page 11). Fold over and serve at once.

Haddock soufflé omelette

cooking time: about 5 minutes

you will need for 2 servings:

3 eggs	1 teaspoon chopped
3 tablespoons cooked	parsley
smoked haddock	salt, Cayenne pepper
lemon juice	1 oz. butter

1 Separate eggs, beat yolks, add fish, flaked very finely.
2 Add lemon juice to taste, parsley, small pinch salt and Cayenne.
3 Beat egg whites stiffly and fold into mixture.
4 Heat butter in an omelette pan and, when just frothy, pour in the egg mixture. Stir until it begins to set and brown underneath, then put under the grill to finish cooking.

Italian omelette

cooking time: about 10 minutes

you will need for 4 servings:

12 oz. courgettes	salt, pepper
1½ tablespoons fresh	pinch sugar
breadcrumbs	4 eggs
2½ tablespoons milk	1 oz. butter
3 tablespoons grated	
Parmesan cheese	

1 Wipe the courgettes and cut into dice.
2 Bring 1¼ pints of salted water to the boil. Blanch the courgettes for 3 minutes. Leave to drain thoroughly.
3 Put breadcrumbs in a large bowl with milk, allow to soak for 5 minutes.
4 Add the courgettes, cheese, salt, freshly ground black pepper and sugar.
5 Beat the eggs until just blended, stir into the courgette mixture.

6 Heat the butter in a large heavy pan, pour in the egg and courgette mixture.
7 Cook over a moderate heat for 4–5 minutes until the eggs are firm, but still lightly moist.
8 Slide the pan under a very hot grill for 30 seconds – to brown the top lightly.
9 Cut the omelette into wedges and serve at once.

Variation

With tomato sauce – made from fresh or canned Italian tomatoes or see page 91, makes a good accompaniment.

Spanish omelette

cooking time: about 10 minutes

you will need for 4 servings:

1 oz. butter	2 tablespoons cooked
1 small onion, peeled	peas
and chopped	4 eggs
1 small cooked potato,	salt, pepper
cubed	paprika
2 tomatoes, peeled and	
chopped	

1 Heat butter in a frying pan.
2 Add onion, potato, tomatoes and peas and sauté for 5 minutes, or until the onion is tender.
3 Pour off any surplus fat.
4 Beat eggs, add seasoning and pour over vegetables.
5 Cook until mixture is just set, then turn upside down on to a hot dish and sprinkle with paprika.

Omelette cardinale

cooking time: 10 minutes

you will need for 4 servings:

1 orange	1 oz. butter
4 eggs	6 oz. prawns
salt, pepper	1 tablespoon single cream

1 Peel the orange very thinly and cut the peel into strips. Remove the pith from the orange and slice thinly.
2 Whisk the eggs and add the seasoning.
3 Heat the butter in a frying pan and pour in the egg mixture. As it begins to thicken, break up the cooked surface with a fork. Continue until the mixture is delicately set, with no liquid part left.
4 Before folding the omelette, fill with half the orange strips and half the prawns mixed with the cream.
5 Fold the omelette and slide on to a serving dish. Arrange orange slices and remaining prawns around the dish and sprinkle the rest of the orange strips on top.
6 Cut into 4 portions and serve.

Vegetable omelette

cooking time: 10–15 minutes

you will need for 3 servings:

2–3 cooked potatoes	1 dessertspoon fresh
1 onion	chopped mixed herbs
1 red or green pepper	or pinch dried mixed
2–3 tablespoons oil	herbs
1 tablespoon cooked	4 eggs
peas, carrots or beans,	salt, pepper
as available	

1 Slice potatoes, peel and chop onion. Remove seeds and pith from pepper and chop finely.
2 Heat the oil in a pan, add potatoes, onion and pepper and cook altogether until the potato and onion have browned.
3 Add the rest of the vegetables and herbs.
4 Beat the eggs, add seasoning and pour over the vegetables.
5 Cook until the omelette is set underneath, then put under a hot grill and brown the top.
Serve at once with green salad.

Tomato and cheese omelette

cooking time: 6–7 minutes

you will need for 2 servings:

2–3 tomatoes	1 tablespoon grated
½ oz. butter	cheese
salt, pepper	3 eggs
pinch sugar	2 tablespoons water
little chopped basil or	butter for frying
oregano	

1 Peel and slice tomatoes and cook for a few minutes in butter.
2 Add seasoning, sugar, herbs and cheese and keep hot.
3 Beat eggs with water and seasoning and make the omelette in the usual way (see page 11).
4 Put tomato mixture in the centre, fold over and serve at once.

Main course dishes

Cauliflower cheese puff

cooking time: 35–40 minutes

you will need for 4 servings:

1 medium-sized	cinnamon
cauliflower	2 eggs
¼ pint thick cheese sauce	2 tablespoons grated
(see page 91)	cheese
salt, pepper	

1 Steam cauliflower and rub through a sieve.
2 Add purée to cheese sauce, season carefully and add a good pinch cinnamon.
3 Separate eggs, stir yolks into the cauliflower mixture.
4 Beat whites stiffly and fold lightly into mixture.
5 Turn into a buttered fireproof dish, sprinkle with cheese and bake in a moderate oven (350°F. – Gas Mark 4) for 35–40 minutes.

Bacon apple grill

cooking time: 20 minutes

you will need for 4 servings:

4 gammon rashers	1 large cooking apple
8 oz. cheese, finely grated	1 oz. Demerara sugar
¼ pint cider	

1 Trim the fat off the bacon, cook under the grill until tender, turning rashers once during cooking.
2 Meanwhile, put the cheese into a saucepan with the cider and melt it over a very low heat, stirring all the

time. After it has melted, continue stirring until the mixture gradually thickens.
3 Peel and cut the apple into twelve sections, removing the core. Sprinkle sections lightly with the sugar and put them under a hot grill for a few minutes on each side to heat and lightly caramelise them.
4 Serve the bacon rashers garnished with apple and accompanied by cheese sauce and sauté or creamed potatoes.

Cauliflower palermo

cooking time: about 25 minutes

you will need for 4 servings:

1 cauliflower	4–6 shrimps, fresh,
1 oz. cornflour	canned or frozen
½ pint tomato juice	1 oz. butter
salt, pepper	4 oz. grated cheese
pinch sugar	lemon juice

1 Prepare cauliflower, divide into flowerets and cook in boiling salted water until just tender (avoid over-cooking). Drain and save ¼ pint water.
2 Put cauliflower into a buttered fireproof dish and keep hot.
3 Blend cornflour smoothly with a little tomato juice. Put the rest on to heat with cauliflower water.
4 Add mixed cornflour, stir till boiling and boil for 3 minutes.
5 Add seasoning, sugar, shrimps, butter, most of the

cheese and a squeeze lemon juice. Mix all well and correct seasoning.

6 Pour sauce over cauliflower, sprinkle with remaining cheese and brown under the grill.

Mixed vegetable platter

cooking time: 40 minutes

you will need for 4 servings:

1 small firm cauliflower	4 tablespoons fresh
12 young carrots	breadcrumbs
6 oz. mushrooms	½ pint cheese sauce (see
3 oz. butter	page 91)
1 packet frozen peas	
1 can asparagus tips, optional	

1 Wash cauliflower, divide into sprigs. Cook in boiling salted water until tender, about 20 minutes. Drain well.
2 Cook carrots in boiling salted water until tender, 20–30 minutes. Drain well.
3 Keep vegetables warm, if necessary.
4 Meanwhile, fry mushrooms gently in half the butter.
5 Cook and drain peas. Toss in ½ oz. butter.
6 Drain asparagus and heat through in ½ oz. of remaining butter. Fry crumbs in remaining butter.
7 Arrange vegetables on a large serving dish with cauliflower in the centre.
8 Pour cheese sauce over the cauliflower, sprinkle carrots with buttered crumbs and serve.

Celery au gratin

cooking time: about 30 minutes

you will need for 4 servings:

2 heads celery	4 oz. grated cheese
¾ pint white sauce (see page 91)	4 oz. breadcrumbs
1 egg	salt, pepper, Cayenne pepper

1 Prepare celery, remove the coarse outer sticks, wash thoroughly.
2 Put into boiling salted water and cook gently for 8–10 minutes.
3 Drain well and cut into pieces.
4 While celery is cooking, make sauce, cool a little and add beaten egg.
5 Mix cheese and breadcrumbs and add seasoning.
6 Put a layer of celery into a buttered fireproof dish. Cover with sauce and sprinkle with cheese and breadcrumbs.
7 Continue in layers till ingredients are used up, finishing with cheese and breadcrumbs.
8 Dot with butter and brown under the grill.

Baked marrow

cooking time: about 1 hour

you will need for 4 servings:

1 vegetable marrow	pinch dry mustard
1 small onion, minced	12 oz. minced cooked
1 teaspoon chopped parsley	meat
pinch salt and pepper	½ pint thick cheese sauce (see page 91)

1 Wash and peel the marrow keeping it whole. Cut a wedge off the top lengthways.
2 Stir the onion, parsley, salt and pepper and the mustard into the meat. Bind with about 1 tablespoon of the sauce.
3 Put the stuffing into the marrow and replace the wedge.
4 Wrap in foil and place on a baking sheet.
5 Bake in a very moderate oven (325°F. – Gas Mark 3) until tender.
6 Remove the foil carefully and place the marrow in a warm dish.
7 Pour on remaining cheese sauce, heated through.

Cheese and mushroom risotto

cooking time: 30 minutes

you will need for 4 servings:

2 oz. butter	1½ pints stock
1 small onion, peeled and chopped	4 tablespoons grated Parmesan cheese
2 oz. mushrooms, sliced	salt, pepper
6 oz. rice	

1 Melt 1 oz. butter, add onion and fry for a few minutes.
2 Add mushrooms and rice and mix well.
3 Add stock and stir till boiling, then cook gently until rice is tender and stock absorbed.
4 Add remaining butter and cheese and correct seasoning. Serve very hot.

Cheese and onion pudding

cooking time: about 20 minutes

you will need for 4 servings:

8 oz. onions	4 oz. grated cheese
1 pint milk	salt, pepper
6 oz. fresh breadcrumbs	Cayenne pepper
3 eggs	chopped parsley

1 Peel and slice onions thinly and cook slowly in milk until just tender.
2 Remove from heat, add breadcrumbs and beaten eggs and most of the cheese.
3 Season very carefully with salt, pepper and a little Cayenne pepper.
4 Turn into a greased fireproof dish, sprinkle with the remaining cheese and bake about 20 minutes in a

moderate oven (350°F. – Gas Mark 4). Serve sprinkled with parsley.

Curried eggs

cooking time: about 1 hour

you will need for 6 servings:

for the sauce:	1 tablespoon mango
4 oz. onions	chutney
2 oz. butter	1 tablespoon brown sugar
8 oz. cooking apples	1 oz. sultanas
2 tablespoons curry	2 tablespoons lemon juice
powder	salt, Cayenne pepper
1 can tomato juice, made	
up to ¼ pint with water	6 oz. Patna rice
	6 hard-boiled eggs

1 Peel and slice onions thinly.
2 Heat butter, add onions, cover and sauté gently for about 10 minutes.
3 Add apples, peeled and chopped, and continue to sauté a further 10 minutes.
4 Add curry powder, mix in well and cook for 5 minutes.
5 Add all other sauce ingredients, cover and simmer gently for about 30 minutes, stirring occasionally.
6 Cook rice in boiling salted water for 12 minutes or until tender. Drain, rinse in hot water.
7 Pile rice on to a hot dish, halve eggs and arrange on top. Correct seasoning of the sauce and pour over the eggs.

Eggs au gratin soubise

cooking time: 15–20 minutes

you will need for 4 servings:

4 eggs	salt, pepper
1 lb. onions	½ oz. flour
3 oz. butter	½ pint milk
4 oz. grated cheese	pinch marjoram
2 oz. breadcrumbs	

1 Cook eggs in boiling water for 6 minutes. Plunge into cold water and remove shells carefully.
2 Peel and slice onions and cook for 5 minutes in boiling salted water. Drain and chop finely.
3 Melt 2 oz. butter, add onion and cook till soft, but not coloured.
4 Mix cheese and breadcrumbs and put half in the bottom of a buttered fireproof dish.
5 Cover with half the onion and sprinkle with salt and pepper. Arrange eggs on top.
6 Make sauce with ½ oz. butter, flour and milk. Add seasoning and marjoram, pour over eggs.
7 Cover with remaining onion and lastly sprinkle on the rest of the cheese and breadcrumbs.
8 Dot with remaining butter and brown in a hot oven (425°F. – Gas Mark 7) for a few minutes.

Cheese and tomato charlotte

cooking time: 20–25 minutes

you will need for 4 servings:

6 oz. grated cheese	12 oz. tomatoes
2 oz. breadcrumbs	salt, pepper, allspice
½ oz. butter	toast

1 Mix cheese and breadcrumbs and put a layer into the bottom of a buttered fireproof dish.
2 Peel and slice tomatoes and put a layer over cheese and breadcrumbs.
3 Sprinkle lightly with seasonings.
4 Continue in layers until ingredients are used up, finishing with cheese and breadcrumbs.
5 Dot with butter and bake in a slow oven (300°F. – Gas Mark 2) for 20–25 minutes.
Arrange some small triangles of toast round the dish before serving.

Eggs bonne femme

cooking time: 25 minutes

you will need for 4 servings:

1½ oz. butter	**for the topping:**
8 oz. onions, peeled and	1 oz. butter
sliced	1 clove garlic
2 teaspoons wine vinegar	3 oz. fresh breadcrumbs
4 eggs	4 oz. grated cheese,
salt, pepper	preferably Parmesan

1 Heat butter and fry onion until golden brown.
2 Stir in vinegar and turn into a buttered fireproof dish.
3 Break eggs carefully and arrange on top of onion. Season lightly.

To make topping

1 Melt butter, add the garlic and heat gently for 5 minutes then remove.
2 Add breadcrumbs and stir over low heat, until a pale brown colour.
3 Mix in the cheese and sprinkle over the eggs.
4 Bake in a moderate oven until the eggs are set (350°F. – Gas Mark 4) about 10 minutes.

Egg and cheese croquettes

cooking time: 5–7 minutes

you will need for 4–6 servings:

1½ oz. butter	2 hard-boiled eggs,
1½ oz. flour	chopped
½ pint milk	2 rashers bacon, grilled
2 eggs	and chopped
salt	egg and breadcrumbs for
pepper	coating
2 oz. breadcrumbs	fat for frying
4 oz. grated cheese	

1 Melt butter, add flour and mix well.
2 Add milk gradually, stir till boiling and boil for 2 minutes.

3 Remove from the heat, beat in eggs and add seasoning, breadcrumbs, cheese, hard-boiled eggs and bacon.

4 Mix well and turn out on to a wetted plate.

5 Smooth top and leave to get cold.

6 Divide into 8 equal portions and shape into croquettes.

7 Coat with egg and breadcrumbs and fry in hot fat. Serve hot with tomato sauce (see page 91) and creamed potatoes, or cold with salad.

Eggs florentine

cooking time: 10–15 minutes

you will need for 4 servings:

1½ lb. fresh spinach or 1 large carton frozen spinach	1 oz. butter
	4 hard-boiled eggs
	½ pint cheese sauce (see page 91)
salt	1 tablespoon grated cheese
pepper	
nutmeg	

1 Cook spinach, drain thoroughly, chop, then add seasoning, good pinch nutmeg and butter.

2 Put spinach into a fireproof dish; slice eggs and arrange on top.

3 Cover with cheese sauce, sprinkle with grated cheese and brown under the grill.

Egg and ham charlotte

cooking time: 20 minutes

you will need for 4 servings:

3 oz. breadcrumbs	salt, pepper
8 oz. ham, chopped finely	4 hard-boiled eggs, sliced
¼ pint cheese sauce (see page 91)	1 oz. butter

1 Grease a pie dish and sprinkle thickly with breadcrumbs.

2 Mix ham with sauce and correct seasoning.

3 Put half the mixture into pie dish and add 2 of the sliced hard-boiled eggs. Cover with remaining meat mixture and put remaining egg slices on top.

4 Cover with the rest of the breadcrumbs, dot with butter and cook about 20 minutes in a moderate oven (350°F. – Gas Mark 4).

Egg and mushroom au gratin

cooking time: about 15 minutes

you will need for 6 servings:

8 eggs	salt, pepper
1½ oz. butter	3–4 tablespoons grated Parmesan cheese
8 oz. mushrooms, sliced	
¼ pint white sauce (see page 91)	

1 Put eggs into boiling water and boil gently for 6 minutes. Put into cold water for a few minutes, then shell carefully.

2 Heat butter, add mushrooms; sauté till tender.

3 Make white sauce, season, and add mushrooms.

4 Chop eggs coarsely and stir into sauce.

5 Reheat, then pour into a fireproof dish.

6 Sprinkle with cheese and brown under the grill.

Egg and ham cutlets

cooking time: about 10 minutes

you will need for 3–4 servings:

1 oz. butter	1 teaspoon chopped parsley
1 oz. flour	
½ pint milk	egg and breadcrumbs for coating
3 hard-boiled eggs	
3 oz. chopped cooked ham	fat for frying
2 oz. breadcrumbs	tomato sauce (see page 91)
little made mustard	
salt, pepper	

1 Make a thick sauce with butter, flour and milk and cook well.

2 Add eggs, chopped finely, ham and breadcrumbs. Mix all well, add seasoning and parsley.

3 Turn on to a wetted plate, spread evenly and mark into 6–8 equal portions. Leave to get cold.

4 Form each into a cutlet shape with floured hands.

5 Coat with egg and breadcrumbs and fry in deep fat. Serve with tomato sauce.

Eggs mornay

cooking time: 30–40 minutes

you will need for 4 servings:

1 lb. potatoes	1 blade mace
1½ oz. butter	¾ oz. flour
¾ pint milk	2 oz. grated cheese
salt, pepper	½ teaspoon French mustard
1 slice onion	
6 peppercorns	4 eggs
1 bay leaf	mashed potato

1 Cook potatoes in boiling salted water till tender. Drain well, and beat with ½ oz. butter and ¼ pint hot milk. Season carefully and arrange down the centre of a fireproof dish. Keep warm.

2 Put remaining milk into a pan with onion, peppercorns, bay leaf and mace. Heat very slowly until flavourings are infused. Strain.

3 Make a sauce with remaining butter, flour and flavoured milk.

4 Add most of the cheese, mustard and seasoning.

5 Poach eggs and arrange on bed of potato.

6 Cover with sauce, sprinkle with remaining cheese and brown under the grill.

Egg and mushroom cream

cooking time: about 15 minutes

you will need for 4 servings:

1 oz. butter	1 can condensed mush-
1 onion, peeled and	room soup
chopped	¼ pint milk
½ teaspoon dry mustard	6 oz. grated cheese
pinch savory or mixed	4 hard-boiled eggs
herbs	toast or French bread

1 Heat butter and sauté onion until golden brown.
2 Add mustard and herbs and mix well with onion.
3 Add mushroom soup, milk and cheese and stir over gentle heat, until cheese has melted and sauce is smooth.
4 Slice eggs and fold carefully into sauce. Serve with fingers of toast or French bread.

Eggs and mushrooms hollandaise

cooking time: about 25 minutes

you will need for 4 servings:

8 oz. mushrooms	¼ pint water
6 oz. butter	lemon juice
4 whole eggs	1 tablespoon bread-
4 egg yolks	crumbs
salt, pepper	

1 Cook mushrooms in about 2 oz. butter, then put into a shallow fireproof dish.
2 While mushrooms are cooking, poach whole eggs and arrange carefully on top of mushrooms.
3 Melt remaining butter.
4 Lightly beat egg yolks then gradually stir in melted butter and seasoning.
5 Gradually add boiling water.
6 Put basin over a pan of hot water, making sure that the water does not touch the bottom of the basin.
7 Stir till sauce thickens, then remove from heat and add lemon juice to taste.
8 Pour sauce over eggs, sprinkle with breadcrumbs, dot with butter and brown under the grill.

Egg and mushroom ragoût

cooking time: 10–15 minutes

you will need for 4 servings:

12 oz. mushrooms	pinch nutmeg
small nut butter	pinch mixed herbs
water	little oil
¼ pint white wine	6 hard-boiled eggs
salt, freshly ground black	
pepper	

1 Pick out and reserve a few of the best mushrooms.
2 Chop the rest coarsely, put into a pan with butter and a little water and bring to the boil.
3 Add wine, seasoning and herbs and cook for about 5 minutes.
4 Brush remaining mushrooms with oil and grill.

5 Chop eggs coarsely while they are still hot and put into a serving dish.
6 Pour mushroom ragoût on top and garnish with grilled mushrooms. Serve at once.

Eggs parmentier

cooking time: 10 minutes, after the potatoes are cooked

you will need for 4 servings:

2 large baked potatoes	1 tablespoon grated
salt, pepper	cheese
¼ pint cheese sauce (see	1 dessertspoon bread-
page 91)	crumbs
4 eggs	½ oz. butter

1 While potatoes are still hot, cut in half length-wise and scoop out some of the inside. Sprinkle potato cases with a little salt and pepper.
2 Put a spoonful of sauce into each case; poach eggs and place one in each case.
3 Cover with sauce.
4 Mix cheese and breadcrumbs and sprinkle on top.
5 Dot with butter and put into a fairly hot oven to brown (400°F. – Gas Mark 6), about 10 minutes.

Potato garnish – the potato that has been scooped out can be beaten with a very little butter and milk, seasoned and rolled into small balls. Coat with flour and brown in the oven. These make a delicious garnish.

Eggs portugaise

cooking time: 40 minutes

you will need for 4 servings:

1 medium onion	1 teaspoon castor sugar
1 medium green pepper	1 teaspoon
2 tablespoons olive or	Worcestershire sauce
corn oil	2 teaspoons lemon juice
2 sticks celery	salt, pepper
2 level tablespoons flour	6 hard-boiled eggs
1 14-oz. can tomatoes	6 oz. rice or noodles

1 Slice onion finely, cut pepper into thin rings or strips. Heat oil and fry onion and pepper, until soft, but not brown.
2 Add celery, cook for further 2 minutes.
3 Stir in flour, allow to cook for 3 minutes without browning.
4 Add tomatoes, sugar, Worcestershire sauce, lemon juice and salt and pepper to taste.
5 Bring to the boil, reduce heat, cover and simmer for 30 minutes, stirring occasionally.
6 Meanwhile, hard-boil eggs and cook rice or noodles. Shell eggs, cut in half lengthwise.
7 Drain rice or noodles and arrange in a warm serving dish.
8 Place eggs on top. Coat with sauce. Serve at once.

18

Variation

Eggs creole – prepare as before, omitting pepper. Add well drained contents of can of sweet corn with peppers, to sauce, after it has come to the boil.

Egg and spaghetti rissoles

cooking time: about 10 minutes

you will need for 4 servings:

1 16-oz. can spaghetti in tomato sauce	1 tablespoon finely chopped parsley
½ small onion, peeled and finely chopped	egg and breadcrumbs for coating
2 oz. flour	deep fat for frying
2 hard-boiled eggs	
1 tablespoon grated cheese	

1 Turn spaghetti into a saucepan and break it into small pieces.
2 Add onion and mix in flour smoothly.
3 Stir over gentle heat until mixture thickens, then add chopped hard-boiled eggs, cheese and parsley. Correct seasoning.
4 Turn out on to a wetted plate and leave to cool.
5 Divide into portions and shape into rissoles on a floured board.
6 Coat with egg and breadcrumbs and fry very quickly in hot fat.

Ham and egg pudding

cooking time: 20–25 minutes

you will need for 4 servings:

4 oz. cooked ham	½ pint milk
3 oz. fresh breadcrumbs	1 oz. butter
pinch finely chopped chervil	salt
4 eggs	pepper

1 Chop ham and mix with breadcrumbs and chervil.
2 Separate the eggs.
3 Heat milk and pour over beaten egg yolks. Add butter and seasoning and mix with ham and breadcrumbs.
4 Beat egg whites till fluffy and fold into mixture.
5 Pour into a buttered fireproof dish and bake about 20–25 minutes in a slow oven (300°F. – Gas Mark 2).

Macaroni cheese

cooking time: about 30 minutes

you will need for 4 servings:

4 oz. macaroni	salt, pepper
1 oz. butter	½ teaspoon made mustard
1 oz. flour	6 oz. grated cheese
1 pint milk plus water in which macaroni has been cooked	toast
	4 grilled or baked tomatoes

1 Cook macaroni in boiling salted water till tender. Drain and reserve 1 pint of the water.

2 Make a sauce with butter, flour and the water. Add seasoning and most of the cheese.
3 Stir in macaroni, then pour into a buttered fireproof dish. Sprinkle remaining cheese on top and brown under the grill or in the oven.
4 Garnish with toast, cut into triangles or half-moon shapes and serve with tomatoes.

Variation

With bacon – add 4 rashers bacon, lightly fried and chopped.

Flemish eggs

cooking time: 10 minutes

you will need for 6 servings:

6 eggs	4 oz. shrimps
¾ oz. butter	salt
1 dessertspoon French mustard	pepper
1 tablespoon chopped parsley	3–4 tablespoons cream
	1½ oz. grated cheese

1 Put eggs into boiling water and boil gently for 6 minutes. Put into cold water for a few minutes, then carefully remove shells.
2 Put eggs on to a plate and chop coarsely.
3 Heat butter in a shallow pan, add eggs, mustard, parsley and shrimps.
4 Stir lightly, add seasoning and cream.
5 Shake pan over moderate heat for a few minutes, then turn contents into a buttered fireproof dish.
6 Sprinkle with the grated cheese, brown under grill.

Scandinavian steakburgers

cooking time: 8–10 minutes

you will need for 4 servings:

2 oz. butter	1 large packet steakburgers
2 oz. Danish blue cheese	

1 Cream the butter and blend with the cheese. Leave in a cool place until required.
2 Grill the steakburgers until tender.
3 Place on a hot dish and top each with a pat of the butter mixture.
4 Garnish with watercress and serve with French fried potatoes.

Macaroni and sausage loaf

cooking time: 40 minutes

you will need for 4 servings:

4 oz. macaroni	2 eggs
½ pint white sauce (see page 91)	salt, pepper
4 oz. grated cheese	1 lb. chipolata sausages
	fat for frying

1 Cook macaroni in boiling salted water till tender, then drain well. *continued*

2 Make white sauce, add macaroni, cheese, beaten eggs and seasoning.

3 Fry sausages till lightly browned, then arrange side by side in a buttered loaf tin.

4 Put macaroni mixture in the centre, cover with buttered paper and bake about 40 minutes in a moderate oven (350°F. – Gas Mark 4).

Macaroni and sausage cheese

cooking time: 15–20 minutes

you will need for 4 servings:

3 oz. macaroni	2–3 tomatoes
¾ pint cheese sauce (see page 91)	2 tablespoons grated cheese
1 8-oz. can cocktail sausages	

1 Cook the macaroni in boiling salted water till tender. Drain well.

2 Make cheese sauce, add macaroni and pour into a fireproof dish.

3 Drain sausages and arrange on top with the peeled and sliced tomatoes.

4 Sprinkle with cheese and put into a moderate oven (350°F. – Gas Mark 4) to heat through for about 10 minutes.

Savoury sausage meringue

cooking time: about 15 minutes

you will need for 4 servings:

1½ oz. butter	4 eggs
4 oz. mushrooms	salt
1 lb. cooked sausages	pepper
6 oz. grated cheese	

1 Melt butter and sauté mushrooms for a few minutes.

2 Cut sausages into pieces and arrange in a fireproof dish in layers with the mushrooms and most of the cheese.

3 Separate eggs, whip whites stiffly, add seasoning and remaining cheese.

4 Pile meringue on top of sausages and make four hollows in it.

5 Put an egg yolk into each hollow, and put into a fairly hot oven (400°F. – Gas Mark 6) for 10–15 minutes till meringue is set and lightly browned.

Scrambled eggs palermo

cooking time: about 20 minutes

you will need for 4 servings:

4 oz. noodles	pepper
4 eggs	¼ teaspoon made mustard
4 tablespoons milk	2 oz. butter
salt	3 oz. grated cheese

1 Cook noodles in boiling salted water till tender.

2 When almost ready, beat eggs and milk together, add salt, pepper and mustard.

3 Heat 1½ oz. butter, scramble the eggs in the usual way (see page 5).

4 Strain noodles, add cheese and remaining butter and toss over gentle heat for a few minutes.

5 Arrange noodles in a border round the serving dish and pile scrambled egg in the centre.

Spaghetti à la russe

cooking time: 20 minutes

you will need for 4 servings:

1 lb. spaghetti	2 hard-boiled eggs
3 oz. butter	3 oz. grated cheese
2 tablespoons cream	2 tablespoons bread-crumbs
salt, pepper	

1 Cook spaghetti in boiling salted water, drain well.

2 Add 2 oz. butter, cream and seasoning and put into a buttered casserole.

3 Arrange sliced hard-boiled eggs on top and cover with cheese.

4 Fry breadcrumbs till brown in remaining butter and sprinkle over cheese.

5 Cook about 20 minutes in a slow oven (275°F. – Gas Mark 1).

Stuffed eggs with tomato sauce

cooking time: 10–15 minutes

you will need for 6 servings:

6 hard-boiled eggs	**for the sauce:**
1 oz. butter	1 oz. butter
1 small onion, peeled and chopped	1 small onion, peeled and chopped
2 oz. mushrooms, chopped	1 stick celery, chopped
salt, pepper	½ small green pepper, seeded and chopped
	½ pint tomato juice
4 rashers streaky bacon for garnish	1 dessertspoon cornflour
	pinch sugar
	salt, pepper

1 Halve eggs lengthwise, remove yolks and rub through a sieve.

2 Heat butter, fry onion and mushrooms till tender.

3 Mix with egg yolk, season carefully and fill egg cases.

4 Arrange eggs on a serving dish and keep hot.

To make the sauce

1 Heat butter and fry onion, celery and green pepper.

2 Add tomato juice and simmer till the vegetables are tender.

3 Blend cornflour smoothly with a little cold water, add to tomato juice, stir till thickened, then boil for 2 minutes.

4 Add sugar, salt, pepper and pour over eggs.

5 Grill bacon and use to garnish the dish.

Spanish eggs

cooking time: 25–30 minutes

you will need for 4 servings:

1 oz. butter	8 oz. tomatoes, peeled
1 onion, peeled and	and chopped
chopped	¼ pint chicken stock
4 oz. lean streaky pork	salt, pepper
1 oz. cooked ham	4 eggs
1 oz. flour	

1 Melt butter, add onion and cook till transparent.
2 Add pork and ham cut into small pieces and continue cooking until onion is golden brown.
3 Stir in flour and mix well.
4 Add tomatoes and stock, stir till boiling then simmer till mixture is quite thick, about 15 minutes.
5 Add seasoning and put mixture into a fireproof dish.
6 Break eggs on top and cook in a moderate oven (350°F. – Gas Mark 4) for about 10 minutes or till the eggs are set.

Spanish scramble

cooking time: 15–20 minutes

you will need for 2 servings:

3 oz. spaghetti	3 eggs
1 green pepper	2 tablespoons milk
2 tablespoons oil	salt, pepper
1 onion, peeled and	
chopped	

1 Cook spaghetti in boiling salted water.
2 Meanwhile, seed and core the pepper and chop finely.
3 Heat the oil, add pepper and onion and sauté till tender.
4 When the spaghetti is cooked, drain well, chop if necessary and add to pepper and onion.
5 Beat eggs, add milk and seasoning and pour over spaghetti.
6 Stir over low heat until eggs are set. Serve hot.

Stuffed eggs au gratin

cooking time: 10 minutes

you will need for 6 servings:

6 hard-boiled eggs	¼ pint cheese sauce (see
1 can sardines	page 91)
1 teaspoon capers,	2 tablespoons bread-
chopped	crumbs
squeeze lemon juice	½ oz. butter
salt, pepper	

1 Halve eggs lengthwise and remove yolks.
2 Drain sardines and reserve the oil.
3 Bone the sardines and mash with egg yolks.
4 Add capers, lemon juice, seasoning and enough oil from the sardines to make a smooth paste.

5 Fill egg whites with mixture and arrange in a fireproof dish.
6 Pour sauce over, cover with breadcrumbs and dot with butter.
7 Put in a moderately hot oven to brown the top (375°F. – Gas Mark 5) for 10 minutes.

Surprise eggs

cooking time: 5–7 minutes

you will need for 4 servings:

4 hard-boiled eggs	salt, pepper
1 oz. butter	egg and breadcrumbs for
¾ oz. cornflour	coating
6 tablespoons milk	fat for frying
1½ oz. grated Parmesan	¼ pint cheese sauce (see
cheese	page 91)

1 Halve eggs lengthwise, remove yolks, sieve.
2 Melt butter, add cornflour and mix well. Add milk and stir until mixture boils. Continue cooking until it leaves the side of the pan clean.
3 Add cheese, seasoning and sieved egg yolk.
4 Fill egg whites with mixture and reshape.
5 Coat with egg and breadcrumbs and fry in deep fat. Serve hot with cheese sauce.

Liver and rice mould

cooking time: 1½ hours

you will need for 4 servings:

1 hard-boiled egg	1 small onion,
6 oz. raw minced liver	chopped
3 oz. boiled rice	1 teaspoon marjoram
3 oz. shredded suet	salt, pepper
1 egg	milk or stock for binding
[2 tomatoes, skinned and	
chopped	

1 Chop the hard-boiled egg and mix with all the other ingredients, binding with a little milk or stock.
2 Press into a greased basin, cover with greased paper and steam.
3 Serve with tomato sauce or a good brown gravy.

Stuffed ham rolls

cooking time: 5–7 minutes

you will need for 4 servings:

4 oz. fresh breadcrumbs	4 oz. grated cheese
¼ pint hot milk	2 eggs
4 oz. mushrooms	salt, pepper
1 oz. butter	4 thin slices ham

1 Put breadcrumbs into a basin, pour on hot milk and leave for 5–10 minutes.
2 Drain and press to remove excess moisture, then mash well with a fork.
3 Chop mushrooms finely and sauté for a few minutes in butter. *continued*

4 Add bread, 2 oz. cheese and well beaten eggs. Mix well and add seasoning. Cook over a low heat for 5 minutes, cool slightly.

5 Put some mixture on each slice of ham and roll up.

6 Put into a fireproof dish, sprinkle with remaining cheese and put into a fairly hot oven (400°F. – Gas Mark 6) for about 5 minutes.

To use remaining stuffing – any remaining stuffing can be rolled into small balls and arranged round the rolls of ham.

Beef and spaghetti

cooking time: 1½–2 hours

you will need for 6 servings:

1½ lb. blade or chuck steak	¼ level teaspoon pepper
1 lb. tomatoes (fresh or canned)	2 level teaspoons salt
	4 oz. spaghetti
1 onion	½ pint stock
2 oz. fat	4 oz. cheese, grated
¼ level teaspoon ground mace	

1 Cut the steak into small cubes.

2 Slice the tomatoes, peel and slice the onion.

3 Melt the fat and fry the steak until brown.

4 Put in a pan with the tomatoes, onion, mace, and seasoning. Simmer for 1–1½ hours.

5 Add the spaghetti, broken into pieces, and stock.

6 Cook slowly for a further 30 minutes until beef and spaghetti are both tender.

7 Just before serving, stir in the grated cheese.

Monday pie

cooking time: 1 hour

you will need for 4 servings:

4 eggs	2 oz. grated cheese
1 lb. potatoes	salt, pepper
2 tomatoes	horseradish sauce or mustard
8 oz. cooked meat	
¼ pint white sauce (see page 91)	

1 Hard-boil the eggs, shell and cut into slices when cold.

2 Cook potatoes, drain well and cut into slices while hot. Skin tomatoes and chop roughly and chop or slice meat.

3 Arrange eggs, potatoes and meat in layers in a greased ovenproof dish. Finish with a layer of potatoes.

4 Add 1½ oz. of cheese to the white sauce. Season well with salt and pepper, adding mustard or horseradish sauce to taste.

5 Pour sauce over the potatoes in the dish. Arrange chopped tomatoes around the edge of the dish. Sprinkle with remaining cheese.

6 Bake in a moderately hot oven (375°F. – Gas Mark 5) for 45 minutes.

Beef au gratin

cooking time: 25–30 minutes

you will need for 4 servings:

1–1½ lb. chopped beef	stock
good pinch thyme	seasoning
1 onion	1½ lb. creamed potatoes
1½ oz. margarine	2 oz. grated cheese
1 dessertspoon tomato purée	2 oz. breadcrumbs

1 Season the meat and add the thyme.

2 Chop the onion and fry in the margarine until soft.

3 Add the beef and tomato purée and enough stock to just cover the meat, bring to the boil. Season.

4 Transfer to a greased ovenproof dish, cover with potato.

5 Sprinkle with a mixture of cheese and breadcrumbs and bake in a moderately hot oven (400°F. – Gas Mark 6) until golden.

Chicken and macaroni

cooking time: about 1 hour

you will need for 2 servings:

3 oz. macaroni	8 oz. cooked chicken, diced
½ small onion, peeled and grated	½ teaspoon paprika
2–3 cooked carrots, diced	2 eggs
salt, pepper	½ pint milk
½ small green pepper, seeded and chopped	

1 Cook macaroni in boiling salted water till tender, then drain well.

2 Add onion, carrot, seasoning, green pepper, chicken and paprika. Mix all well and put into a buttered casserole.

3 Beat eggs, add milk and pour over mixture.

4 Cover and stand casserole in a pan of hot water.

5 Cook for about 1 hour in a slow oven (325°F. – Gas Mark 3).

Hot tumble

cooking time: about 30 minutes

you will need for 4 servings:

2 oz. dripping	salt, pepper
2 onions, finely chopped	pinch mixed herbs
4 large cooked potatoes, chopped	4 eggs
1–1½ lb. cooked meat (beef, pork or lamb) cut into cubes	parsley

1 Heat the dripping and fry the onions until tender.

2 Add potatoes and cook until golden brown, add meat and season with salt, pepper and the mixed herbs.

3 Cook until thoroughly heated, adding more fat if necessary to prevent the mixture from sticking to the pan.

4 Transfer to a shallow warmed dish.

5 Fry the eggs and place on top of the meat.

6 Garnish with parsley and serve at once.

Moussaka

cooking time: 50 minutes

you will need for 4 servings:

2 Spanish onions	2 tablespoons tomato
1–2 cloves garlic,	purée
optional	¼ pint stock
7–8 tablespoons olive or	salt, pepper
corn oil	3 aubergines
1 lb. cooked lamb	3 tablespoons flour
4 oz. mushrooms	2 oz. cheese
4 tomatoes	3 eggs
2 tablespoons chopped	1 5-fl. oz. carton natural
parsley	yoghurt

1 Slice onions, peel and chop garlic, fry in 4 tablespoons of the oil for 10 minutes, without browning.

2 Mince or finely chop the lamb. Mix with the mushrooms and tomatoes, skinned and chopped, adding the parsley.

3 Add to the onion mixture in the pan. Stir in the tomato purée and stock, and cook gently for 10 minutes. Season to taste with salt and pepper.

4 Slice unpeeled aubergines, lengthwise, dust with flour. Fry in 3 tablespoons oil until golden brown on both sides. Drain well.

5 Grate cheese.

6 Place a layer of aubergine in the bottom of an ovenproof dish. Cover with meat and vegetable mixture.

7 Top with remaining slices of aubergine. Sprinkle with half the grated cheese.

8 Beat the eggs together, beat in the yoghurt and pour over the contents of the dish. Sprinkle with remaining cheese.

9 Bake in a moderate oven (350°F. – Gas Mark 4) for 30 minutes, until the top is lightly browned.

Parmesan veal

cooking time: 20 minutes

you will need for 4 servings:

4 oz. white breadcrumbs	4 loin veal chops
1 tablespoon chopped	salt
parsley	pepper
2 oz. grated Parmesan	1 egg
cheese	2 oz. butter

1 Mix together breadcrumbs, parsley and cheese.

2 Sprinkle chops lightly with salt and pepper.

3 Beat egg with 2 tablespoons water.

4 Dip chops into beaten egg, coat with cheese and crumb mixture. Melt butter, cook chops over a moderate heat until tender, about 10 minutes each side.

Pork chops Milanese

cooking time: 1¼ hours

you will need for 4 servings:

4 pork chops	½ small onion, peeled
salt, pepper	and minced
3 tablespoons oil	½ clove garlic, minced
1½ oz. breadcrumbs	1 can peeled tomatoes
2 oz. grated cheese	

1 Trim chops, season and brush both sides with oil.

2 Mix breadcrumbs and cheese together and coat chops with mixture.

3 Heat oil, add onion and garlic and brown lightly.

4 Add chops and brown on both sides then transfer all to a casserole.

5 Add tomatoes, cover and cook about 1¼ hours in a slow oven (325°F. – Gas Mark 3). Correct seasoning before serving.

Steak fondue

cooking time: about 20 minutes

you will need for 4 servings:

1½ lb. rump steak	salt
4 oz. Lancashire or	paprika pepper
Cheddar cheese	mustard
3–4 tablespoons sherry	broccoli or mushrooms
	for serving

1 Prepare steak and grill or fry.

2 Meanwhile, heat cheese in a basin over a pan of hot water until the cheese has melted.

3 Gradually add the sherry, stirring throughout.

4 Season to taste with salt, pepper and mustard.

5 Pour cheese over the steak and serve, accompanied with cooked broccoli or mushrooms.

Veal in cream sauce with cheese

cooking time: 30 minutes

you will need for 4 servings:

1 onion, sliced	1–5 fl. oz. carton soured
1 oz. butter	cream
2 tablespoons corn oil	4 oz. Parmesan cheese,
1½ lb. frying veal	grated or Gruyère,
salt, pepper	sliced

1 Fry the onion lightly in the butter and oil. Add the veal, and cook until browned.

2 Pour in the cream and season to taste with salt and pepper. Cover with grated or sliced cheese.

3 Bake for 20 minutes at 375°F. – Gas Mark 5. Brown under a hot grill.

Veal Mozzarella

cooking time: 1 hour

you will need for 4 servings:

4 escalopes veal	2 rashers streaky bacon, chopped
1 oz. cornflour	
salt, pepper	8 oz. tomatoes, peeled and sliced
1 egg, beaten	
breadcrumbs	8 oz. Mozzarella cheese, sliced
2 tablespoons corn oil	
1 small onion, chopped	1 oz. Parmesan cheese, grated
1 clove garlic, crushed (optional)	

1 Cut each escalope of veal into 4 pieces.
2 Toss in cornflour, to which salt and pepper have been added. Coat with egg and breadcrumbs.
3 Lightly fry the veal until golden brown – remove from pan and keep hot.
4 Sauté the onion, garlic, if used, bacon and tomato for 5 minutes.
5 Place half the veal in the bottom of an ovenproof dish, cover with half the tomato mixture and the Mozzarella cheese. Add remaining veal and tomato mixture.
6 Sprinkle with Parmesan cheese, and bake for 45 minutes at 325°F. – Gas Mark 3.
7 Flash under a hot grill to brown before serving.

Veal – Swiss style

cooking time: 30 minutes

you will need for 4 servings:

4 veal cutlets	2 level tablespoons flour
oil	freshly ground pepper
4 oz. Cheddar cheese	8 oz. tomatoes, peeled
2 level teaspoons French mustard	watercress

1 Brush cutlets lightly with oil. Place on rack and grill under a moderate heat until cooked through – about 20 minutes. Turning once.
2 Meanwhile, grate cheese, mix with mustard, flour and a sprinkle of pepper.
3 Chop tomatoes roughly and mix with cheese.
4 Drain cutlets, place in a shallow flameproof dish. Spread cutlets with cheese mixture.
5 Return to the grill and grill until cheese is golden brown and bubbling.
6 Garnish with watercress.

Tomato and egg risotto

cooking time: 25–30 minutes

you will need for 4 servings:

4 oz. rice	4 oz. grated cheese
1 oz. butter	3–4 anchovy fillets
2 tablespoons finely chopped onion	salt
	pepper
1 oz. flour	4 eggs
1 can tomato soup	

1 Cook rice in boiling salted water, then drain.
2 Melt butter and fry onion till soft but not coloured. Add flour and mix well.
3 Add soup, stir till boiling.
4 Add most of the rice and cheese, chopped anchovy fillets and seasoning as required.
5 Turned into a fireproof dish. Make four hollows and break an egg into each.
6 Sprinkle with remaining cheese and bake in a moderate oven until the eggs are set (350°F. – Gas Mark 4), about 10 minutes.

Casseroles

Bacon and potato casserole

cooking time: 25–30 minutes

you will need for 4 servings:

1 lb. cooked potatoes	3 hard-boiled eggs, sliced
4 oz. rashers streaky bacon	½ oz. breadcrumbs
	½ oz. butter
¼ pint yoghurt or sour milk	

1 Slice potatoes and put half of them into a greased casserole.
2 Cover with half the bacon rashers pour on half the yoghurt and cover with half the eggs.
3 Continue in layers, finishing with potatoes.
4 Sprinkle breadcrumbs over and dot with butter.
5 Put into a slow oven (325°F. – Gas Mark 3) for 30 minutes until top is nicely browned.

Egg and celery casserole

cooking time: 15–20 minutes

you will need for 4 servings:

1½ oz. butter	4 oz. grated cheese
1 medium-sized onion, peeled and chopped	3–4 tablespoons cooked peas
1 can condensed celery soup	4 hard-boiled eggs
3 tablespoons milk	1 tablespoon bread-crumbs

1 Melt ¾ oz. butter, add onion and cook till soft but not coloured.

2 Add soup, milk and most of the cheese.

3 Stir over low heat for 3–4 minutes.

4 Add peas, chopped eggs; put in buttered fireproof dish.

5 Mix remaining cheese with breadcrumbs and sprinkle on top.

6 Dot with butter and put into a moderate oven (350°F. – Gas Mark 4) for 15–20 minutes.

Egg and cheese casserole no. 1

cooking time: 30 minutes

you will need for 4 servings:

2 oz. spaghetti	salt, pepper
4 eggs	4 oz. cooked ham,
1 oz. butter	chopped
¾ oz. cornflour	1 tablespoon bread-
1 pint stock	crumbs
4 oz. grated cheese	

1 Cook spaghetti in boiling salted water.

2 Boil eggs for 6 minutes, plunge into cold water for a few minutes, then shell carefully.

3 Melt butter, add cornflour and mix well. Add stock gradually, stir till boiling and boil for 3 minutes. Remove from heat and add cheese, reserving 1 tablespoon.

4 Season sauce to taste and put about ⅓ into a buttered casserole.

5 Add half the spaghetti, eggs and ham and cover with half the remaining sauce.

6 Put remaining spaghetti on top and then add remaining sauce.

7 Mix breadcrumbs with the spoonful of cheese and sprinkle on top.

8 Put into a moderate oven (350°F. – Gas Mark 4) till well browned.

Egg and cheese casserole no. 2

cooking time: 20 minutes

you will need for 6 servings:

3 medium-sized onions	2 tablespoons cornflour
1 oz. butter	4 oz. grated cheese
¼ pint water	Cayenne pepper
salt, pepper	1 tablespoon bread-
½ pint milk	crumbs
6 hard-boiled eggs	1–2 tomatoes

1 Peel and slice onions and put into a pan with the butter and water. Add a little seasoning and cook until onions are soft and transparent.

2 Strain off the liquor and add to the milk.

3 Arrange layers of onion and sliced hard-boiled egg in a buttered casserole.

4 Blend cornflour smoothly with a little of the milk and onion water. Put the rest on to heat. Add mixed cornflour and stir till boiling. Boil for 3 minutes.

5 Add most of the cheese, seasoning and a pinch Cayenne pepper and pour into casserole.

6 Sprinkle with remaining cheese mixed with breadcrumbs.

7 Peel and slice tomatoes thickly and arrange round the edge of the dish.

8 Cook about 20 minutes in a moderate oven (350°F. – Gas Mark 4).

Egg and cheese casserole no. 3

cooking time: about 40 minutes

you will need for 4 servings:

4 tomatoes	3 oz. grated cheese
salt, pepper	1½ lb. creamed potatoes
sugar	4 rashers streaky bacon
4 eggs	
¼ pint thick white sauce (see page 91)	

1 Cut tomatoes into thick slices and sprinkle with salt, pepper and a little sugar.

2 Hard-boil the eggs and slice them.

3 Make the sauce. Stir in the cheese and season to taste.

4 Pipe or spread the creamed potato round the inside edge of a greased casserole.

5 Arrange the sliced hard-boiled eggs in the bottom of the dish.

6 Place tomatoes round the edge next to the potato and pour in cheese sauce.

7 Lay the rashers of bacon across the top. Cook under a hot grill 10–15 minutes. If the dish is prepared in advance, heat through in a moderate oven (350°F. – Gas Mark 4) for 20–30 minutes.

Ham, egg and sweet corn casserole

cooking time: 15 minutes

you will need for 4 servings:

1 tablespoon corn oil	1 11-oz. can corn kernels
1 oz. cornflour	2–3 oz. ham, chopped
1 chicken stock cube	3 hard-boiled eggs,
¼ pint milk	shelled and quartered
¼ pint water	1 tablespoon bread-
3 oz. grated cheese	crumbs

1 Heat corn oil, add cornflour and stock cube and mix well.

2 Add milk and water, stir till boiling and boil for 1 minute.

3 Remove from heat, add cheese (reserving 1 tablespoon) sweet corn and ham.

4 Place eggs in a buttered casserole.

5 Pour sauce mixture on top.

6 Mix remaining cheese and breadcrumbs and sprinkle on top.

continued

7 Bake for 15 minutes in a moderate oven (350°F. – Gas Mark 4), then brown under the grill.

Cheese and onion casserole

cooking time: 1 hour

you will need for 4 servings:

6 slices white bread, from a large loaf	¼ level teaspoon salt
6 oz. grated Lancashire cheese	1 small onion, finely grated
2 standard eggs	½ pint milk
	pepper

1 Trim crusts off bread. Cut each slice into 2 triangles.

2 Arrange half the pieces of bread over the base of a shallow buttered ovenproof dish.

3 Cover bread with 4 oz. of the grated cheese. Top with remaining pieces of bread.

4 Beat eggs, add salt and onion.

5 Heat milk until almost to boiling point. Pour on to the eggs, stirring all the time. Add pepper to taste.

6 Pour into dish, over the bread and cheese. Leave to stand for 30 minutes. Sprinkle over 2 oz. cheese.

7 Bake in the centre of a moderate oven (350°F. – Gas Mark 4) for 50 minutes – 1 hour, until golden brown.

Pork and macaroni casserole

cooking time: about 1 hour

you will need for 4 servings:

4 oz. macaroni	2 sticks celery, chopped finely
3 oz. butter	
4 pork chops	6 oz. grated cheese
½ oz. flour	salt, pepper
½ pint milk	4 oz. mushrooms, sliced
1 small onion, peeled and chopped	

1 Cook macaroni in boiling salted water.

2 Heat 1½ oz. butter and fry chops until brown.

3 Make a sauce with remaining butter, flour and milk.

4 Add onion, celery, cheese and seasoning and cook till cheese has melted. Add macaroni and mushrooms.

5 Pour sauce into a casserole and arrange chops on top. Cover and cook in a slow oven (325°F. – Gas Mark 3) about 1 hour. Add a little extra milk or stock if necessary during the cooking.

Savoury egg casserole

cooking time: 20 minutes

you will need for 6 servings:

6 hard-boiled eggs	1 tablespoon bread-crumbs
4 oz. cooked ham	
2 oz. cooked tongue	½ oz. butter
¼ pint white sauce (see page 91)	
3 oz. grated cheese	triangles of toast for garnish
salt, pepper	

1 Slice eggs thickly and place in a casserole.

2 Chop ham and tongue and mix with white sauce.

3 Add 1½ oz. cheese, correct seasoning, then pour mixture over eggs.

4 Mix remaining cheese with breadcrumbs and sprinkle on top.

5 Dot with butter and brown in a hot oven (400°F. – Gas Mark 6).

6 When cooked, arrange toast round the edge of the dish and serve with salad.

Shrimps and rice casserole

cooking time: 40 minutes

you will need for 2 servings:

1 oz. butter	1 tablespoon tomato ketchup
4 oz. mushrooms	
3 oz. rice	½ teaspoon Worcestershire sauce
2 5-oz. cans shrimps or 8 oz. frozen shrimps	
6 oz. grated cheese	salt, pepper
1 6-oz. can cream	potato crisps

1 Heat butter, add sliced mushrooms and sauté till tender.

2 Cook rice in boiling salted water till just tender, then drain.

3 Mix rice, shrimps, cheese and mushrooms.

4 Add cream, ketchup, sauce and seasoning and mix.

5 Turn into a casserole and cook for 40 minutes in a slow oven (325°F. – Gas Mark 3).

6 Remove the lid for the last 5 minutes and sprinkle over crushed potato crisps.

Cottage cheese casserole

cooking time: 40 minutes

you will need for 4 servings:

2 oz. button mushrooms	1½ oz. soft white bread-crumbs
1 oz. butter	
1 small green pepper	8 oz. ham
3 eggs	12 oz. cottage cheese
¼ pint milk	1 teaspoon made mustard
	salt, pepper

1 Slice mushrooms and fry lightly in butter.

2 Cut off stalk end and remove pips from pepper. Cut into thick strips or rings.

3 Place in cold water, bring to the boil. Pour off water and drain well. Keep some pieces of pepper for garnishing, chop remainder roughly.

4 Warm the milk, beat in the eggs and pour over the breadcrumbs. Leave for 10 minutes, add chopped ham then beat all into the cottage cheese.

5 Add the mushrooms and chopped pepper. Mix well and season with mustard, salt and pepper.

6 Pour into a well greased casserole, garnish with strips of pepper and bake in a moderate oven (350°F. – Gas Mark 4) for 30 minutes.

Summer vegetable casserole

cooking time: 25–30 minutes

you will need for 4 servings:

1 lb. mixed cooked vegetables (carrots, peas, beans, potatoes etc., as available)	1½ oz. flour
	½ pint milk
	2 eggs
12 chives	salt, pepper
3½ oz. butter	pinch nutmeg
3 tomatoes	4 oz. grated cheese

Dice carrots and potatoes, chop chives and sauté all the vegetables in 2 oz. butter.

2 Put into a buttered casserole and cover with slices of peeled tomatoes.

3 Heat remaining butter in a pan, add flour and mix well. Add milk and stir till boiling.

4 Separate eggs, stir yolks into sauce and add seasoning, nutmeg and cheese.

5 Beat whites stiffly and fold into sauce.

6 Pour over vegetables; bake in a moderately hot oven (400°F. – Gas Mark 6) for 25 minutes.

Cold dishes

Anchovy eggs

no cooking

you will need for 4 servings:

4–6 hard-boiled eggs	1 teaspoon anchovy essence
1 oz. butter	
2 tablespoons salad cream or mayonnaise (see page 89)	pepper
	salad cress

1 Halve eggs, remove yolks and rub through a sieve.

2 Soften butter a little and beat into yolks.

3 Add salad cream, anchovy essence and a little pepper.

4 Pipe or pile mixture into egg cases.

5 Serve on a bed of salad and sprinkle a little cress on top.

Variation

With curry powder – omit the anchovy essence and add 1 teaspoon curry powder.

Devilled eggs

no cooking

you will need for 4 servings:

6 hard-boiled eggs	1 teaspoon chopped parsley
salt, Cayenne pepper	
pinch sugar	1 teaspoon capers, chopped
½ teaspoon mustard	
2 tablespoons cream	
1 tablespoon vinegar	**for garnish:** watercress

1 Shell and halve the eggs lengthwise.

2 Remove yolks, put into a basin and pound thoroughly with all other ingredients.

3 Correct seasoning and fill egg whites with the mixture. Serve, garnished with watercress, with salad.

Egg croquettes

cooking time: 5–6 minutes

you will need for 4 servings:

1 oz. butter	1 dessertspoon chopped parsley
1 oz. flour	
½ pint milk	4 hard-boiled eggs
1 egg yolk	egg and breadcrumbs for coating
salt, pepper	
1 oz. grated cheese	fat for frying

1 Melt the butter, add flour and mix well.

2 Add milk, stir till boiling and boil for 1 minute stirring all the time.

3 Add yolk, seasoning, cheese, parsley and chopped hard-boiled eggs. Mix all well. Turn out on to a wetted plate, spread smoothly and mark into eight even portions. Leave until cold.

4 Roll each portion into a sausage shape with floured hands.

5 Coat with egg and breadcrumbs and fry in deep fat till golden brown. Serve cold with salad.

Egg and prawn mayonnaise

cooking time: 15 minutes

you will need for 4 servings:

4 oz. rice	paprika
3 tablespoons oil	1 small cucumber
1 tablespoon vinegar	4 hard-boiled eggs
salt, pepper	mayonnaise (see page 89)
pinch sugar	4 oz. shelled prawns

1 Cook rice in boiling salted water till tender. Drain and rinse in cold water.

2 Make a dressing with oil, vinegar, seasoning, sugar and enough paprika to give a faint pink colour.

3 Moisten rice with dressing, arrange on dish.

4 Peel cucumber, cut lengthwise into four and then across in chunks. *continued*

5 Shell and halve eggs, then arrange on the rice. Coat with mayonnaise and garnish the sides of the dish with cucumber and prawns.

Eggs and shrimps in aspic

no cooking

you will need for 4 servings:
½ pint aspic jelly   4 hard-boiled eggs
1 4-oz. can shrimps

1 Make the jelly as instructed on the packet and leave until cold.
2 Put 1 tablespoon jelly into the bottom of each of 8 dariole moulds and leave to set.
3 Arrange a ring of shrimps round the edges and put a slice of egg in the centres. Cover each with another spoonful of jelly and put aside to get quite firm.
4 Fill the moulds with any remaining shrimps and egg and cover with liquid aspic.
5 Leave to set. Turn out and serve with salad.

Fish and cheese mould

cooking time: 1 hour

you will need for 4 servings:
1½ lb. cooked white fish   juice of ½ lemon
4 oz. grated cheese   salt, pepper
½ pint thick white sauce   2 eggs
  (see page 91)   few drops cochineal
1 tablespoon anchovy
  essence

1 Skin and bone the fish; flake finely.
2 Add cheese, white sauce, anchovy essence and lemon juice.
3 Mix all well and correct seasoning.
4 Separate eggs, beat yolks and add to fish mixture.
5 Fold in stiffly beaten whites.
6 Add a few drops of cochineal to give a pale pink colour.
7 Put into a well buttered mould or pudding basin, cover with buttered paper and steam for 1 hour.
8 Leave to get quite cold in the mould, then turn out and serve with salad.

Veal mould

cooking time: 1½ hours

you will need for 6 servings:
1½ lb. breast, shoulder or   bacon or ham bone
  knuckles of veal   2 level teaspoons salt
  (weighed without the   *bouquet garni*
  bone)   1½ pints water
1 carrot   ½ oz. gelatine
1 turnip   2 hard-boiled eggs
1 onion   salt, pepper

1 Wash the meat, then peel the vegetables.
2 Put the veal and bacon or ham bone in a pan with the vegetables, salt, *bouquet garni* and water.

3 Bring to the boil and simmer until the meat is tender – about 1½ hours.
4 Strain and keep the liquid.
5 Cut the meat into small pieces, heat ½ pint of the liquid and dissolve the gelatine in it.
6 Cool until just beginning to set.
7 Mix in the meat, salt and pepper, and the eggs.
8 Pour into a mould which has been rinsed out with cold water, and leave in a cold place until set. Turn out and slice.

Ham and eggs in aspic

no cooking

you will need for 4 servings:
1 pint packet aspic jelly   3–4 stuffed olives
1 can tomato juice   6 oz. cooked ham
2 tablespoons cooked   4 hard-boiled eggs
  peas

1 Put aspic jelly into a basin.
2 Make the tomato juice up to ¾ pint with water. Bring to boiling point, pour over the aspic and stir till dissolved. Leave until cold.
3 Rinse out a charlotte mould or small cake tin with water and put a layer of jelly in the bottom. Leave to set.
4 Moisten peas and sliced olives with a spoonful of the liquid aspic. Arrange peas in a circle round the edge of the tin and then arrange the olive slices in a pattern.
5 Spoon a little more liquid aspic over this decoration and leave to set.
6 Cube the ham and eggs and put into the tin when the decoration is quite set.
7 Fill with liquid aspic and leave to set.
Turn out and serve with salad.

Stuffed tomatoes

no cooking

you will need for 4 servings:
4 large firm tomatoes   2 teaspoons finely
salt, pepper   chopped chives or
4 oz. Gorgonzola or   spring onions
  Danish Blue cheese   Cayenne pepper
1 oz. butter   lettuce

1 Cut a slice from stalk ends of the tomatoes. Vandyke the edge if time permits, then remove the pulp with a small teaspoon. Discard the seeds and chop pulp finely.
2 Sprinkle a little salt and pepper into the tomato cases and leave upside down to drain.
3 Crumble the cheese with a fork, work in the butter then add tomato pulp, chives and a pinch of Cayenne.
4 Pile mixture into tomato cases and serve on a bed of lettuce.

Salads

Apple and prawn salad

you will need for 4 servings:

lettuce	½ pint prawns (fresh,
2 apples	frozen or canned)
2 hard-boiled eggs	mayonnaise (see page 89)
few stuffed olives	lemon juice
few radishes	

1 Line a salad bowl with lettuce, reserving the heart for garnish.
2 Core but do not peel apples, cut into dice.
3 Slice the eggs, olives and some of the radishes but keep one or two for garnish.
4 Mix the prawns with the other ingredients and bind with mayonnaise.
5 Add a little lemon juice and seasoning, if required.
6 Pile on top of the lettuce and garnish with radishes and the lettuce heart.

Beetroot, egg and cheese salad

you will need for 4 servings:

1 lettuce	mayonnaise (see page 89)
1 beetroot	2 oz. grated cheese
4 hard-boiled eggs	watercress
salt, pepper	radishes

1 Shred the outer lettuce leaves and place in a shallow salad bowl.
2 Arrange beetroot slices in a ring round the edge and top with a ring of sliced egg.
3 Chop remaining eggs, add salt and pepper and bind with a little mayonnaise. Pile in the centre of the salad and arrange the lettuce heart around the base.
4 Sprinkle with cheese, garnish with watercress and radishes. Serve extra mayonnaise separately.

Cheese balls and grapefruit salad

you will need for 4 servings:

1 carton cottage cheese	watercress
2 oz. chopped nuts	cucumber
salt, pepper	1 can grapefruit
1 lettuce	

1 Mix cheese and nuts, add seasoning and shape into balls.
2 Arrange lettuce, watercress and sliced cucumber in a salad bowl.
3 Drain the juice from the grapefruit and arrange segments and cheese balls on the salad.
Serve French dressing (see page 90) separately.

Cheese jelly salad

you will need for 4 servings:

8 oz. cottage cheese	salt, freshly ground black
2 oz. Danish Blue cheese	pepper
1 tablespoon chopped	1 teaspoon gelatine
parsley	3 dessertspoons hot
1 tablespoon mayonnaise	water
or salad cream (see	2 tablespoons thick cream
page 89)	green salad
1 teaspoon finely chopped	1 small can pineapple
chives	pieces, drained

1 Mix cottage cheese with crumbled Blue cheese and add parsley, mayonnaise, chives and seasoning. Mix all well together.
2 Dissolve gelatine in the water, cool a little and stir into cheese mixture.
3 Half whip the cream and fold in.
4 Put mixture into a refrigerator tray or a similar container approximately 9-inches × 4-inches × 1-inch and chill overnight. This mixture should not be frozen.
5 When required for use, turn out carefully and cut into 4 or 8 portions.
6 Arrange on a bed of green salad.
7 Chop the pineapple and sprinkle on top.

Cheese and macaroni salad

you will need for 4 servings:

1 lettuce	salt, Cayenne pepper
8 oz. Cheddar cheese	French dressing (see
6 oz. cooked macaroni	page 90)
1 small red pepper	radishes for garnish
few chopped chives	

1 Prepare lettuce and arrange in a salad bowl.
2 Mix grated cheese and macaroni, add seeded and chopped red pepper, chives and seasoning.
3 Add 3–4 tablespoons French dressing and toss all the ingredients lightly.
4 Pile on to lettuce and garnish with radishes cut into roses.

Cheese and pineapple salad

you will need for 4 servings:

6 oz. cottage cheese	1 small can pineapple
2 oz. walnuts or hazel	rings
nuts, chopped	salt, Cayenne pepper
2 tablespoons thick cream	1 lettuce
1 teaspoon lemon juice	paprika

1 Break cheese with a fork and add most of the nuts.
2 Half whip the cream, add lemon juice, 1 teaspoon

pineapple juice and seasoning and mix with cheese.

3 Arrange lettuce in a shallow bowl and pile cheese mixture on top.

4 Arrange rings of pineapple round and sprinkle with remaining nuts and paprika.

Cheese and ham salad

you will need for 4 servings:

1 head lettuce	1 tablespoon vinegar
8 oz. Gruyère cheese	salt, freshly ground black
12 oz. ham	pepper
3 tablespoons oil	chopped parsley

1 Prepare the lettuce.

2 Cut the cheese and ham into dice.

3 Make the dressing and pour over the cheese and ham. Leave to stand for an hour or so in the refrigerator if possible.

4 Pile on top of the lettuce and sprinkle with chopped parsley.

Cheese salad, no. 1

you will need for 4 servings:

1 lettuce	4 oz. tomatoes, skinned
1 bunch watercress	and quartered
French dressing (see page 90)	4 oz. cheese, cubed

1 Wash and dry the lettuce and watercress.

2 Toss in the dressing.

3 Garnish with tomatoes and cheese.

Cheese salad, no. 2

cooking time: 15 minutes

you will need for 4 servings:

4–6 oz. small new potatoes	mayonnaise or salad cream (see page 89)
8 oz. tomatoes	squeeze lemon juice
6–8 oz. cheese (two or more varieties can be mixed)	lettuce watercress chives

1 Cook potatoes in boiling salted water, drain, cool a little, then cut into dice.

2 Peel and slice tomatoes.

3 Dice or crumble the cheese.

4 Bind potatoes, tomatoes, and cheese with mayonnaise or salad cream to which lemon juice has been added.

5 Line a salad bowl with lettuce and watercress, pile cheese mixture in the centre and sprinkle with chopped chives.

Celery and cream cheese salad

you will need for 4 servings:

lettuce	1 tablespoon lemon juice
1–2 heads celery	salt, pepper
4 oz. cream cheese	1–2 gherkins
2 tablespoons salad oil	

1 Arrange the lettuce in a salad bowl.

2 Cut the celery into strips and pile on top of the lettuce.

3 Mix the cream cheese with the oil and lemon juice. Add salt and pepper and the chopped gherkins.

4 Pour over the celery and decorate, if liked, with a few chopped nuts.

Cheese star salad

you will need for 4 servings:

1 lettuce	4 slices processed cheese
2 hard-boiled eggs	4 stuffed olives
2 tomatoes	mayonnaise or salad
watercress	cream (see page 89)

1 Arrange lettuce, eggs, tomatoes and watercress attractively on a large platter.

2 Cut each cheese slice into four diagonally, leaving about 1-inch uncut in the centre.

3 Gather the four alternate points of each slice, put an olive in the centre and secure with a cocktail stick.

4 Arrange on the bed of salad and serve with mayonnaise or salad cream.

Cheese and potato salad

you will need for 4 servings:

1 lb. new potatoes, cooked and sliced	about 6 tablespoons salad dressing
2 finely chopped spring onions or a few chives	8 oz. cheese lettuce
2 teaspoons chopped parsley	tomatoes

1 Slice the potatoes while still hot, add the finely chopped onion or chives, parsley and sufficient salad dressing to coat the potato. Leave until cold.

2 Dice the cheese into very small pieces and lightly toss it into the mixture.

3 Serve piled in the centre of a plate of crisp lettuce and garnish with tomato quarters.

Cream cheese and apple salad

you will need for 4 servings:

2 oz. cream cheese	2 hard-boiled eggs
2 tablespoons mayonnaise (see page 89)	2 small apples 1 lettuce salad dressing (see page 89)
½ small onion, minced or finely chopped	

1 Mix cheese with mayonnaise.

2 Add onion, 1 chopped egg and 1 apple, peeled, cored and chopped.

3 Toss lettuce lightly with salad dressing and arrange in a salad bowl.

4 Pile cheese mixture in the centre.

5 Garnish with remaining egg and apple, both sliced.

Cottage salad

you will need for 4 servings:

6 oz. cottage cheese	**for the dressing:**
salt, freshly ground black pepper	2 tablespoons oil
1 teaspoon chopped chives	2 dessertspoons wine vinegar
1 oz. walnuts or hazel nuts	2 teaspoons lemon juice
4 oranges	pepper, salt
2 grapefruit	pinch sugar
chopped parsley or mint	

1 Mix cheese with salt, pepper, chives and chopped nuts. Shape into balls and chill.

2 Peel oranges and grapefruit and cut into segments free from skin or pith.

3 Mix all ingredients for the dressing, pour over the fruit and leave to marinate for about 30 minutes.

4 Arrange the fruit on a dish. Put the cheese balls on top and sprinkle with parsley, or arrange three or four small mint leaves on the fruit.

Egg and anchovy salad

you will need for 4 servings:

1 lettuce	radishes
4 hard-boiled eggs	watercress or mustard and cress
mayonnaise (see page 89)	
1 small can anchovy fillets	

1 Prepare the lettuce and arrange in a shallow bowl.

2 Halve eggs lengthwise and arrange on the lettuce.

3 Coat each egg with mayonnaise.

4 Put anchovies in a criss-cross pattern over the eggs.

5 Slice radishes, put in a ring round each egg. Serve garnished with watercress or mustard and cress.

Egg and cheese salad clamart

you will need for 4 servings:

1 lettuce	mayonnaise (see page 89)
4 hard-boiled eggs	4 oz. cream cheese
cooked green peas	cress for garnish

1 Prepare the lettuce and put it into a shallow salad bowl.

2 Halve eggs lengthwise and remove yolks.

3 Mix peas with a little mayonnaise and pile into egg cases. Arrange on lettuce.

4 Beat egg yolks and cheese and add enough mayonnaise to bind. Correct seasoning and form the mixture into balls.

5 Arrange on the salad and garnish with a little cress. Serve with extra mayonnaise.

Cream cheese and pear salad

you will need for 4 servings:

2 large ripe pears or 1 small can pears	2 oz. chopped walnuts
	salt
lemon juice	pepper
4 oz. cream cheese	1 lettuce
1–2 sticks celery, chopped finely	salad dressing (see page 89)

1 Peel, halve and core the pears. Scoop out a little of the flesh from the centre of the fruit and put it into a bowl.

2 Sprinkle pears with lemon juice.

3 Mix cream cheese, chopped celery and most of the walnuts with pear flesh. Add seasoning and mix well.

4 Put a spoonful into the hollow of each pear and roll the rest into small balls. Roll in the remaining nuts.

5 Shred the outer lettuce leaves and place on a serving dish. Arrange pears and the little balls on top.

6 Garnish with lettuce heart and serve the dressing separately.

Italian salad

you will need for 4 servings:

4 oz. cooked rice	salt, pepper
1 tablespoon tomato purée	2 hard-boiled eggs, sliced
6 oz. cooked cold beef	French dressing (see page 90)
4 oz. Bel Paese cheese	paprika or chopped parsley
2 gherkins	

1 Mix rice with tomato purée.

2 Cut meat and cheese into strips and mix with rice.

3 Add chopped gherkins and seasoning.

4 Arrange mixture on a serving dish and put sliced egg round the edge.

5 Pour a little dressing over the top and sprinkle with paprika or parsley.

Mixed salad

you will need for 4 servings:

1 lettuce	8 oz. cold cooked meat, ham, tongue or chicken as available
2 hard-boiled eggs	
3–4 tomatoes	watercress
4 oz. Cheddar cheese	French dressing (see page 90) or salad cream

1 Prepare lettuce and arrange on a shallow dish.

2 Quarter the eggs and cut tomatoes in wedges.

3 Cut cheese and meat into strips and arrange in little heaps on the lettuce. *continued*

4 Put eggs and tomatoes in between.

5 Garnish with sprigs of watercress. Serve the dressing or salad cream separately.

Peach cheese salad

you will need for 4 servings:

1 lettuce	1 oz. chopped nuts
4 fresh peaches or 1 can peach halves	6–8 chives, chopped salt, Cayenne pepper
4 oz. cottage cheese	black grapes

1 Prepare lettuce and arrange on a platter.

2 If fresh peaches are used, peel, halve and remove the stones.

3 Scoop out a little of the flesh from each half and mix with cheese.

4 Add nuts, chives and seasoning.

5 Pile mixture on to the peaches and garnish with grapes. Serve on the bed of lettuce.

Philadelphia salad

you will need for 4 servings:

1 large red pepper	3–4 chives, chopped finely
1 large green pepper	2–3 olives, chopped finely
4 oz. cream cheese	mayonnaise (see page 89)
3 tablespoons chopped nuts	seasoning
3–4 sticks celery, chopped finely	1 lettuce
1 tablespoon chopped parsley	1–2 tomatoes
	1 hard-boiled egg

1 Slice the stem end of each pepper and remove the core and seeds.

2 Mix cheese, nuts, celery, parsley, chives and olives.

3 Bind with mayonnaise and correct seasoning.

4 Stuff peppers tightly with this mixture and put aside to chill.

5 When ready to serve, slice peppers and arrange on a bed of lettuce.

6 Garnish with alternate slices of tomato and egg.

Prawn and egg salad

you will need for 4 servings:

endive or lettuce	few radishes
1 pint prawns (fresh, frozen or canned)	capers
3 hard-boiled eggs, sliced	French dressing

1 Arrange the endive or lettuce round a flat serving dish.

2 Arrange the prawns and slices of egg neatly in layers.

3 Garnish with radishes and capers and serve the dressing separately.

Salad americana

you will need for 4 servings:

1 lettuce	1–2 sticks celery, chopped
4 oz. cream cheese	2 tablespoons thin cream
1 oz. chopped walnuts	1 dessertspoon lemon juice
½ level teaspoon celery salt	1 orange

1 Arrange the lettuce in a fairly shallow bowl.

2 Mix together the cheese, walnuts, celery salt, celery, cream, lemon juice and pile in the centre of the lettuce.

3 Peel the orange, removing as much of the pith as possible.

4 Divide into segments and arrange round the salad.

Salad caprice

you will need for 4 servings:

1 carton cottage cheese	1–2 bananas, peeled
2 oz. chopped nuts	lemon juice
2–3 tablespoons chopped pineapple	French dressing (see page 90)
1 lettuce	watercress
1 grapefruit	

1 Mix cheese with nuts and pineapple.

2 Arrange lettuce in a shallow bowl and pile cheese on top.

3 Divide grapefruit into segments, slice bananas and sprinkle with lemon juice.

4 Arrange fruit around cheese and pour dressing on top.

5 Decorate with sprigs of watercress.

Swiss salad

you will need for 4 servings:

8 oz. Gruyère cheese	lettuce
8–12 oz. cooked ham	few black olives
4–5 tablespoons French dressing (see page 90)	

1 Dice cheese and ham.

2 Pour the dressing over and leave in a cold place for about 1 hour.

3 Prepare lettuce and arrange in a salad bowl. Pile cheese and ham on top and garnish with olives.

Salad niçoise

you will need for 4 servings:

¼ small clove garlic	2 hard-boiled eggs, sliced
½ lettuce	1 7-oz. can tuna fish
1 head chicory	French dressing
2 tomatoes, peeled and quartered	1 small can anchovy fillets
small pieces cucumber, sliced	few black olives, optional

1 Rub round the salad bowl with the cut clove of garlic.

2 Shred the lettuce, divide the spears of chicory and put into the salad bowl with the tomatoes, cucumber and eggs.

3 Drain excess oil from the fish, divide into 4 portions and put on top of the salad.

4 Pour over the dressing and garnish with anchovy fillets and olives.

Vegetarian salad

you will need for 4 servings:

1 lettuce	4 oz. cream cheese
2 large fresh pears or 1	2 oz. dates, chopped
small can	1 oz. walnuts, chopped
lemon juice	seasoning

1 Prepare the lettuce, shred the outer leaves and keep the heart for garnish. Put the shredded lettuce on to a serving dish.

2 Peel and halve the pears, remove the core and a little of the flesh.

3 Sprinkle the pears with lemon juice.

4 Put the flesh cut from the pears into a bowl with the cheese, dates and nuts and mix well. Add seasoning as required.

5 Pile a little on each pear and roll the rest into small balls.

6 Arrange the pears and the balls on the lettuce and decorate with the heart of the lettuce.

7 Serve salad dressing separately.

Summer salad

cooking time: 12 minutes

you will need for 4 servings:

4 oz. Patna rice	4 oz. cooked ham
1 small can pineapple	mayonnaise (see page 89)
8 oz. cheese	watercress

1 Cook the rice in boiling salted water till tender. Drain well, rinse in warm water and leave to cool.

2 Arrange rice in a ring on a serving dish, and moisten with a little pineapple juice.

3 Chop pineapple, leaving a few larger pieces for garnish.

4 Cut cheese and ham into 1-inch cubes.

5 Mix chopped pineapple, cheese and ham, and bind with mayonnaise.

6 Pile in the centre of the rice ring.

7 Garnish with remaining pineapple and sprigs of watercress. Serve with a green salad.

Desserts

Cooked

Apple meringue

cooking time: about 20 minutes

you will need for 4 servings:

1 lb. cooking apples	1 strip lemon peel
¼ pint water	2 oz. semolina
4 oz. sugar	2 eggs, separated

1 Peel apples, put into pan with water, 2 oz. sugar and lemon peel, cook till tender.

2 Remove peel and beat well or, preferably, rub through a sieve.

3 Measure quantity of purée and make up to 1¼ pints with water or fruit juice.

4 Return to pan, add semolina and cook gently until semolina is soft and transparent.

5 Remove from heat, add beaten egg yolks, a little extra sugar if required and pour into a fireproof dish.

6 Beat egg whites stiffly, fold in remaining sugar and pile on top of pudding.

7 Put into a very moderate oven (325°F. – Gas Mark 3) for about 20 minutes or until meringue is set and lightly browned.

Apricot dreams

cooking time: 15–20 minutes to cook apricots

you will need for 4 servings:

8 oz. dried apricots	2 eggs
3 oz. sugar	1 6-oz. can evaporated
1 lemon jelly	milk

1 Soak apricots overnight in enough water to cover.

2 Simmer in water until tender, add the sugar. Sieve or beat until smooth.

3 Dissolve jelly in a little hot water, stir into apricot purée. Make up to ¾ pint with water.

4 Separate eggs. Pour apricot mixture on to yolks, stirring well.

5 Whisk milk, chilled if possible, until thick.

6 Whisk whites until stiff.

7 Whisk whites and milk into jelly.

8 Taste, add more sugar if required.

9 Pile into 4 individual glasses, decorate with spikes of blanched almonds, if liked.

Apple condé

cooking time: 25–30 minutes

you will need for 4 servings:

4 oz. rice	sugar
1½ pints milk	1 oz. butter
1 lb. apples	2 eggs, separated

1 Wash rice and cook slowly in milk.
2 Peel and core apples and cook with a little water and sugar to taste.
3 Put stewed apple into a buttered fireproof dish.
4 When rice is tender, remove from heat and add butter and egg yolks.
5 Spread rice over apples.
6 Beat egg whites stiffly, beat in 2 tablespoons sugar and pile on top of the rice.
7 Bake in a slow oven (325°F. – Gas Mark 3) till crisp and golden brown.

Apple custard

cooking time: about 40 minutes

you will need for 4 servings:

2 small sponge cakes	1 egg
1 large apple baked and sieved or 1 small can apple purée	1 tablespoon sugar
	¼ pint milk

1 Crumble the sponge cakes into a small pie dish.
2 Cover with sieved apple pulp.
3 Beat egg with sugar.
4 Warm the milk and pour over the egg mixture.
5 Strain over apple and leave to stand about 10 minutes.
6 Bake in a slow oven (325°F. – Gas Mark 3) until set and lightly browned.
7 Serve either hot or cold, with extra cooked apple, if liked.

Apple flummery

cooking time: 20–25 minutes

you will need for 4 servings:

1 pint milk	1 4½-oz. can apple purée
1 oz. semolina	lemon juice
pinch salt	cochineal (optional)
2 eggs	
2 oz. sugar	**to decorate:**
	glacé cherries
	angelica

1 Warm milk, sprinkle in semolina and stir till boiling. Add salt and cook gently for about 10 minutes, stirring from time to time.
2 Separate eggs, cream yolks and sugar and stir into semolina. Cook a further few minutes without boiling. Remove from heat.

3 Add apple purée, lemon juice and cochineal.
4 Beat egg whites stiffly and fold into mixture.
5 Put into individual glasses and chill before serving. Decorate with cherries and angelica.

Baked banana custard

cooking time: about 30 minutes

you will need for 4 servings:

3 bananas	3 eggs
squeeze lemon juice	1 oz. sugar
1 pint milk	cinnamon

1 Peel bananas, mash, add lemon juice and beat to a pulp.
2 Put milk on to heat.
3 Beat eggs and sugar together, add banana pulp and warm milk.
4 Pour into a buttered pie dish and sprinkle with cinnamon.
5 Stand the dish in baking tin of cold water and bake in a slow oven (300°F. – Gas Mark 2) till firm.

Banana cream

cooking time: about 10 minutes

you will need for 4 servings:

3 bananas	sugar
little apricot jam	½ pint milk
1 lemon	2 eggs

1 Halve bananas lengthwise and sandwich with a little jam. Put into a serving dish.
2 Sprinkle with lemon juice and sugar.
3 Put milk on to heat slowly with a few strips of thinly pared lemon rind.
4 Separate eggs, beat yolks with 1 dessertspoon sugar.
5 Strain milk on to yolks, return to pan and cook over gentle heat till custard thickens. Leave to cool a little, then pour over the bananas. Leave to get cold.
6 Beat egg whites stiffly, beat in 1½ tablespoons sugar and pile on top.

Baked dumplings

cooking time: 8–10 minutes

you will need for 4 servings:

4 oz. flour (with plain flour use ¾ teaspoon baking powder)	1½ teaspoons sugar
	1 egg
2 oz. shredded suet	milk
	jam or syrup

1 Mix all the ingredients together, adding enough milk to give a firm dough.
2 Roll into small dumplings and place in a baking tin containing a little fat.

3 Bake in a moderate oven (350°F. – Gas Mark 4) placing the tin near the top of the oven.

4 Serve hot with jam or syrup.

5 Make sure that the mixture is stiff enough for the dumplings to hold their shape in the baking tin.

Bavaroise

cooking time: 7–10 minutes

you will need for 4 servings:

3 egg yolks	2 tablespoons thick
2 oz. castor sugar	cream
1 teaspoon cornflour	1 egg white
¾ pint milk	3 tablespoons red-
¼ oz. gelatine	currant jelly
1 orange	

1 Beat egg yolks with sugar and cornflour till pale and creamy.

2 Heat milk, pour on to egg mixture, then return to pan and stir over gentle heat until custard thickens.

3 Add gelatine dissolved in a little hot water, strain and leave to cool.

4 Grate rind of orange. Squeeze juice.

5 Add grated orange rind and juice and lightly whipped cream to mixture.

6 Leave until mixture begins to thicken, and stir frequently.

7 Fold in the stiffly beaten egg white, pour into a serving dish and leave to set.

8 Heat jelly with a little water and when just melted, but not hot, pour over the bavaroise.

Butterscotch cream

cooking time: few minutes

you will need for 4 servings:

4 oz. granulated sugar	1 dessertspoon gelatine
5 tablespoons boiling	¼ pint thick cream
water	
3 eggs	**to decorate:**
6 oz. castor sugar	split almonds
1 tablespoon lemon juice	extra cream

1 Put sugar into a small thick saucepan and heat very slowly until it caramelises.

2 Add water and stir until caramel dissolves.

3 Separate eggs, whisk yolks with castor sugar and lemon juice until thick and creamy.

4 Add the caramel, a little at a time, whisking well.

5 Dissolve gelatine in 2 tablespoons hot water and stir into mixture.

6 Fold in stiffly beaten egg whites and lastly whipped cream.

7 Pour into a serving dish and, when set, decorate with almonds and cream.

Brown pudding

cooking time: 2–3 hours

you will need for 4 servings:

4 oz. margarine	4 oz. fresh breadcrumbs
4 oz. soft brown sugar	½ teaspoon sieved
2 eggs	bicarbonate of soda
3 tablespoons golden	pinch salt
syrup	

1 Cream the fat and sugar until light and fluffy.

2 Beat in the eggs and golden syrup.

3 Stir in the breadcrumbs, sieved bicarbonate soda and salt.

4 Put into a greased basin, cover with a greased paper and steam.

5 Serve with golden syrup.

Bread pudding

cooking time: 1½ hours

you will need for 4 servings:

4 oz. stale breadcrumbs	2 oz. sugar
2 oz. flour (with plain	½–1 oz. candied lemon
flour use ½ teaspoon	peel or marmalade
baking powder)	¼ teaspoon allspice
3 oz. shredded suet	¼ teaspoon cinnamon
2 oz. currants	2 eggs
2 oz. raisins	milk to mix

1 Mix all the dry ingredients together in a bowl.

2 Add the beaten eggs and enough milk to give a dropping consistency.

3 Turn into a greased basin, cover with greased paper and steam.

Variation

Baked bread pudding – prepare as before making the mixture slightly more moist. Turn into a greased pie dish and bake in the centre of a moderate oven (350°F. – Gas Mark 4) for about 1 hour. If preferred, the pudding can be cooked at 300°F. – Gas Mark 2 – for about 2 hours.

Turn out of the dish and serve with custard, rum sauce or lemon sauce.

Cabinet pudding

cooking time: 50–60 minutes

you will need for 4 servings:

3 small sponge cakes	½ teaspoon vanilla
2 eggs	essence
1 oz. sugar	fruit purée or jam sauce
½ pint milk	

1 Cut sponge cakes into dice.

2 Beat eggs and sugar together.

3 Heat milk and add to eggs.

4 Add vanilla and pour over diced cakes.

5 Leave until cold. *continued*

35

6 Butter a plain mould or small cake tin and line the bottom with a round of buttered paper.

7 Pour mixture in and steam very gently until firm.

8 Turn out carefully and serve with fruit purée or jam sauce.

Caramel custard

cooking time: 1¼–1½ hours

you will need for 4 servings:

4½ oz. sugar	¼ pint thin cream
¼ pint water	4 eggs
¾ pint milk	vanilla essence

1 Put 4 oz. sugar into a small strong saucepan with water. Heat till sugar has dissolved, then boil until it caramelises.

2 Pour caramel into a 5-inch cake tin or charlotte mould and turn it round until the bottom and sides of the tin are evenly coated.

3 Heat milk, cream and remaining sugar and pour over beaten eggs.

4 Add a few drops of vanilla essence and strain into the prepared tin. Cover with greaseproof paper or aluminium foil.

5 Stand tin in a container with cold water coming about ¼ of the way up the tin and cook for about 45 minutes in a fairly slow oven (325°F. – Gas Mark 3). Then reduce the heat to (275°F. – Gas Mark 1) for a further 40–45 minutes.

To steam – caramel custard may be steamed. Allow water to simmer only and it will take about 1 hour to cook. If the custard is to be served cold, leave in the tin until cold before turning out.

Cheese and apple charlotte

cooking time: 40–45 minutes

you will need for 4 servings:

6 oz. breadcrumbs	1–2 oz. sugar
1 lb. cooking apples, peeled and sliced thinly	4 oz. grated cheese, preferably ½ Parmesan
2–3 sticks celery, chopped	and ½ Cheddar
salt, pepper	2 oz. butter
	3 tablespoons milk

1 Grease a fireproof dish and sprinkle the bottom and sides with breadcrumbs.

2 Put in a layer of apples and some celery.

3 Sprinkle with salt, pepper and sugar and add some cheese. Dot with butter.

4 Repeat layers until ingredients are used up, but reserve 1 tablespoon cheese and 1 tablespoon bread-crumbs and a little butter.

5 Add milk, mix remaining cheese and breadcrumbs and sprinkle on top.

6 Dot with butter, and bake in a moderate oven (350°F – Gas Mark 4) for about 40 minutes.

Cheese bread and butter pudding

cooking time: about 45 minutes

you will need for 4 servings:

4 slices buttered bread	1 egg
3 oz. grated cheese	salt, pepper
½ pint milk	

1 Butter a fireproof dish and arrange alternate layers of bread and cheese, finishing with bread.

2 Heat milk, pour over beaten egg and add seasoning.

3 Strain into dish.

4 Bake in a fairly slow oven (325°F. – Gas Mark 3) until firm and lightly browned.

Cheesecake

cooking time: 40–45 minutes

you will need for 4 servings:

for the crust:	for the filling:
6 oz. digestive biscuits	12 oz. cream cheese
1 oz. sugar	2 eggs
3 oz. butter	2 oz. sugar
	¼ pint sour cream
	vanilla essence

1 Crush biscuits and add sugar.

2 Melt butter and mix with biscuit crumbs.

3 Butter a pie plate and line the bottom and sides with biscuit mixture.

4 Bake for 10 minutes in a moderate oven (350°F. – Gas Mark 4). Remove and leave to cool.

5 Beat cheese and eggs together, add sugar, cream and a few drops of vanilla essence.

6 Pour into the prepared pie plate and bake in a moderate oven (350°F. – Gas Mark 4) for 30–35 minutes or until set. Serve cold.

Chocolate custard

cooking time: about 40 minutes

you will need for 4 servings:

1 tablespoon grated chocolate	¼ oz. sugar
½ pint milk	1 egg
	vanilla essence

1 Heat chocolate with milk and sugar until chocolate has melted and milk is just below boiling point.

2 Beat egg and add chocolate milk slowly, stirring all the time.

3 Add a few drops of vanilla essence and strain into a small buttered fireproof dish.

4 Stand in a dish of cold water and cook in a slow oven (300°F. – Gas Mark 2) until the custard has set.

Chocolate cream

cooking time: 45 minutes

you will need for 4 servings:
½ pint milk	1 oz. sugar
2½ oz. chocolate	few drops vanilla essence
3 eggs	

1 Heat milk, add chocolate and stir till dissolved.
2 Beat eggs thoroughly with sugar.
3 Add milk and vanilla essence and mix well.
4 Pour into a small plain mould or basin, stand the mould in a baking tin of water and cook in a slow oven (300°F. – Gas Mark 2) until quite firm, about 45 minutes. Leave to get cold.

Coconut pyramids

cooking time: 30 minutes

you will need for 4 servings:
2 egg whites	3 oz. desiccated coconut
4 oz. castor sugar	food colouring (optional)
1 teaspoon rice flour	

1 Beat whites until mixture stands up firmly.
2 Sift in 2 oz. sugar and beat till stiff and dry.
3 Using a metal spoon, fold in remaining sugar, rice flour and coconut.
4 Divide mixture into two or three portions and add a few drops of food colouring.
5 Shape into pyramids, put on to a baking tray lined with rice paper and dry off in a slow oven (275°F. – Gas Mark 1) for about 30 minutes.

Baked coconut pudding

cooking time: about 1½ hours

you will need for 4 servings:
2 oz. fresh breadcrumbs	½ pint milk
1 oz. sugar	¾ oz. butter
1 oz. desiccated coconut	1–2 eggs
little grated lemon rind	castor sugar

1 Place the breadcrumbs, sugar, coconut and lemon rind in a bowl.
2 Heat the milk and butter and pour over the dry ingredients. Leave to stand for 5 minutes.
3 Separate eggs and beat yolks.
4 Add the egg yolks and pour into a greased pie dish.
5 Bake in a very moderate oven (325°F. – Gas Mark 3) for about 20–30 minutes until set.
6 Stiffly whisk the whites, add 1½ teaspoons castor sugar to each white and whisk lightly again.
7 Pile the meringue on top of the pudding, sprinkle with coconut and return to a cool oven (200°F. – Gas Mark ¼) until pale brown.

Coffee cream

cooking time: about 10 minutes

you will need for 4 servings:
½ pint milk	
2 eggs	
1½ oz. sugar	
½ oz. gelatine	**to decorate:**
½ teaspoon vanilla	whipped cream
essence	glacé cherries
1 tablespoon coffee	
essence	
¼ pint thick cream	

1 Heat milk.
2 Mix eggs and sugar, add warm milk, return to heat and cook over a pan of hot water until mixture thickens.
3 Remove from heat and leave to cool.
4 Dissolve gelatine in 2 tablespoons hot water, add to custard with vanilla and coffee essence.
5 Half whip the cream and fold into custard mixture when quite cool.
6 Pour into a wetted mould and leave to set.
7 Turn out and decorate with whipped cream and glacé cherries.

Coffee pudding

cooking time: about 40 minutes

you will need for 4 servings:
1 pint milk	¼ pint strong coffee
4 eggs	pinch salt
3 oz. sugar	extra sugar

1 Scald milk, then leave to cool a little.
2 Beat eggs and sugar together, add milk, coffee and salt.
3 Strain into a fireproof dish. Stand dish in a baking tin and half fill the tin with warm water.
4 Bake in a slow oven (300°F. – Gas Mark 2) until the pudding is firm.
5 Leave to cool and sprinkle with sugar before serving.

Cream jelly

cooking time: 20 minutes

you will need for 4 servings:
2 eggs	1 packet jelly
¾ pint milk	1 teaspoon vanilla
3 dessertspoons sugar	essence
pinch salt	

1 Separate the eggs and beat the yolks slightly.
2 Heat the milk, sugar and salt and pour over the egg yolks.
3 Return to the pan and add the jelly, broken into cubes. Bring slowly to the boil until dissolved.
4 Boil until the mixture 'breaks' into curds and whey.
5 Add the vanilla essence.   *continued*

6 Beat the egg whites until stiff and fold into the mixture.

7 Pour into a mould and leave to set.

8 Turn out and serve.

Cream pancakes

cooking time: 2–3 minutes for each pancake

you will need for 4 servings:

4 egg yolks	pinch nutmeg
2 egg whites	butter for frying
¼ pint cream	sugar
1½ oz. butter	lemon slices
3 oz. flour	

1 Beat yolks and whites together.

2 Warm cream and stir into eggs.

3 Add melted butter.

4 Add flour gradually and mix till quite smooth, then add nutmeg.

5 Heat some butter in a small pan and fry the pancakes in the usual way, but they should be very thin. Sprinkle sugar and roll up. Serve with lemon slices.

Cup custard

cooking time: 15–20 minutes

you will need for 2 servings:

2 eggs	¼ pint milk
½ oz. sugar	few drops vanilla essence

1 Beat eggs, sugar and milk together.

2 Add flavouring and strain into well buttered individual basins.

3 Stand on a folded cloth in a pan containing enough boiling water to come half way up the basins. Cover basins with buttered paper.

4 Allow water to simmer very gently for about 15 minutes, when the custard should be firm.

Dolce di semola

cooking time: 15 minutes

you will need for 4 servings:

1 pint milk	grated rind 1 orange
4 oz. fine semolina	(optional)
2 eggs	2 oz. seeded raisins
sugar to taste	fat for frying
grated nutmeg	castor sugar

1 Heat the milk, sprinkle in the semolina and cook stirring until thick.

2 Remove from the heat and beat in the eggs.

3 Sweeten to taste and add the nutmeg, orange rind if used and the raisins. Allow to cool.

4 Using a teaspoon, scoop out nut shaped pieces of mixture and fry in hot deep fat until golden brown.

If preferred they can be shallow fried in butter.

5 Drain on crumpled absorbent paper and serve sprinkled with castor sugar.

Eve's pudding

cooking time: 40–45 minutes

you will need for 4 servings:

1 lb. apples	2 eggs
2 tablespoons water	grated rind ½ lemon
2–4 oz. sugar	4 oz. sieved plain flour
4 cloves (optional)	1 level teaspoon baking
4 oz. butter or margarine	powder
4 oz. castor sugar	

1 Peel, core and slice the apples into a small saucepan. Add the water and the sugar. Add the cloves if used.

2 Cover and cook slowly until the apples are soft, stirring occasionally. When cooked remove the cloves and turn the apples into a greased pie dish.

3 Cream the butter or margarine and the castor sugar until soft and creamy. Beat in the eggs.

4 Add the lemon rind and fold in the flour and baking powder.

5 Mix to a soft consistency and spread the mixture over the apples.

6 Bake in a moderate oven (350°F. – Gas Mark 4) for 40–45 minutes.

Flemish cream

cooking time: few minutes

you will need for 4 servings:

1 teaspoon cornflour	1½ oz. sugar
generous ¼ pint thin	1 small bay leaf
cream	strip lemon peel
3 eggs	2 tablespoons sherry

1 Mix cornflour smoothly with a little of the cream, then add remaining cream.

2 Separate eggs, beat yolks and sugar and mix with cream.

3 Pour into a saucepan, add bay leaf and lemon peel and stir over very gentle heat until mixture is thick enough to coat the back of a spoon.

4 Strain into a basin, add wine and leave to get quite cold.

5 Beat egg whites stiffly and fold lightly but thoroughly into the cream.

6 Pour into glasses and chill very well before serving.

Variation

Madeira cream – ingredients and method as above, substituting 3 tablespoons Madeira for sherry and omitting the bay leaf.

Floating islands

cooking time: about 25 minutes

you will need for 4 servings:

3 eggs	1 pint milk
3 tablespoons sugar	salt

1 Put 1 whole egg and 2 yolks into a basin, add tablespoon sugar and beat till creamy.
2 Warm ½ pint milk, pour on to egg mixture, then return to the pan and cook over very gentle heat until custard thickens.
3 Cool a little, then pour into a serving dish and leave to get cold.
4 Beat the 2 egg whites with a pinch salt till frothy. Add remaining sugar and beat till very stiff to make a meringue.
5 Put remaining milk into a shallow pan and bring to boiling point.
6 Drop meringue in tablespoonfuls into the milk and poach lightly, turning once.
7 Remove carefully and arrange round the custard.

Fruit meringue pudding

cooking time: about 35 minutes

you will need for 4 servings:

stewed or canned fruit as available	4 oz. sugar
	½ pint milk
2–3 sponge cakes	1 teaspoon cornflour
2 eggs	

1 Put some fruit into the bottom of a fireproof dish and cover with thin slices of sponge cake.
2 Pour over just enough fruit juice to moisten the cake.
3 Separate eggs, beat yolks with 1 oz. sugar.
4 Warm milk, add to egg yolks, then return to the pan and cook over gentle heat until custard thickens. Pour custard over the sponge cake.
5 Beat egg whites with a pinch of salt until frothy. Add remaining sugar mixed with cornflour and beat till stiff.
6 Pile meringue on top of the pudding and put into a slow oven (300°F. – Gas Mark 2) until the meringue is crisp and lightly browned.

Ginger cream

cooking time: about 10 minutes

you will need for 4 servings:

¼ pint milk	2 tablespoons ginger syrup
3 egg yolks	
1½ oz. sugar	½ pint thick cream
½ oz. gelatine	1 tablespoon preserved ginger, freshly chopped

1 Warm the milk.
2 Beat egg yolks and sugar until thick and creamy.

3 Add milk, return to pan and stir over gentle heat until custard thickens.
4 Dissolve gelatine in ginger syrup and stir into custard. Leave to cool.
5 Half whip the cream and fold into custard. Stir in ginger.
6 Pour into a wetted mould and leave to set.

Gooseberry meringue

cooking time: about 30 minutes

you will need for 4 servings:

1 lb. gooseberries	2 oz. rice
5 oz. sugar	2 eggs
½ pint water	

1 Cook gooseberries with 3 oz. sugar and the water.
2 When quite soft, rub through a sieve. Measure the quantity of purée and make up to 1¼ pints with water.
3 Return to pan, add rice and cook slowly till tender, stirring occasionally.
4 Remove from heat, stir in egg yolks and sweeten to taste if necessary.
5 Put mixture into a fireproof dish.
6 Beat egg whites till frothy. Add remaining sugar and beat till stiff.
7 Pile on top of pudding and put into a slow oven (300°F. – Gas Mark 2) to set the meringue.

Honeycomb mould

cooking time: about 10 minutes

you will need for 4 servings:

2 large eggs or 3 small eggs	½ teaspoon vanilla essence
1 pint milk	½ oz. gelatine
1½ oz. sugar	2 tablespoons water

1 Separate the eggs. Put milk on to heat.
2 Mix egg yolks and sugar and beat till white and creamy.
3 Add warm milk, return to pan and stir over gentle heat until custard thickens. Remove from heat and add flavouring.
4 Dissolve gelatine in water and stir into custard; allow to cool.
5 Pour into a wetted mould, and leave to set, or pour into a serving dish. Serve with fruit and cream.

Lemon egg jelly

cooking time: 15–20 minutes

you will need for 4 servings:

2 lemons	½ oz. gelatine
water	2 eggs
8 oz. loaf sugar	

1 Wash lemons and peel very thinly, discarding any white pith. *continued*

2 Squeeze juice from lemons and make quantity up to 1 pint with water.

3 Put lemon peel, sugar, lemon juice and water into a pan. Bring slowly to boiling point, then simmer for 10 minutes.

4 Add gelatine and stir till dissolved, then leave to cool a little.

5 Beat eggs and strain liquid on to them.

6 Return to the pan and cook very gently, stirring all the time till the mixture thickens. Do not let the mixture boil or it will curdle.

7 Pour into a wetted mould and leave to set.

Lemon chiffon

cooking time: few minutes

you will need for 4 servings:

¼ pint cold water	2 egg whites
1 lemon	
1 pint lemon jelly tablet	sponge fingers
¼ pint cream	

1 Put water into a pan with 1–2 strips thinly pared lemon rind and lemon juice and bring slowly to the boil.

2 Put jelly tablet into a measuring jug. Strain boiling water on to it and stir till jelly has melted.

3 Make quantity up to ¾ pint with cold water. Pour into basin, leave until beginning to set.

4 Whisk cream until thick, then stir into jelly.

5 Fold in stiffly beaten egg whites.

6 Pile into a glass dish or serve in individual glasses with sponge fingers.

Lemon chiffon pie

cooking time: 30 minutes

you will need for 4 servings:

1 oz. cornflour	2 large lemons
4 oz. sugar	1 oz. butter
2 eggs, separated	1 7-inch baked flan case
½ pint water	(see page 91)

1 Put the cornflour, sugar and egg yolks into a basin. Mix well together and add a little cold water.

2 Heat rest of the water slowly with the thinly pared lemon rind.

3 Strain on to cornflour mixture, return to pan, stir till boiling and cook for 3 minutes.

4 Remove from heat, add lemon juice and butter and leave to cool a little.

5 Beat egg whites stiffly and using a metal tablespoon fold into mixture.

6 Turn into the pastry case and bake in a moderate oven (350°F.–Gas Mark 4) for 30 minutes.

Lemon jelly cream

cooking time: about 15 minutes

you will need for 4 servings:

2 lemons	½ oz. gelatine
½ pint water	2 egg yolks
2 oz. sugar	

1 Wash lemons and peel as thinly as possible. Squeeze out juice.

2 Put peel with water, sugar and gelatine and heat for 5–10 minutes, until gelatine has melted. Do not let mixture boil.

3 Cool a little, then strain over beaten egg yolks stirring all the time.

4 Return to pan and stir over gentle heat with a wooden spoon until mixture thickens. Do not allow it to get too hot otherwise the mixture will curdle.

5 Add strained lemon juice, pour into glasses, and leave to set.

Lemon fluff

cooking time: few minutes

you will need for 4 servings:

2 lemons	¼ oz. gelatine
¼ pint water	2 egg whites
2 oz. sugar	

1 Wash lemons; peel as thinly as possible.

2 Put peel with the water, sugar and gelatine.

3 Heat very slowly until gelatine has melted, strain and leave to cool.

4 Squeeze lemons, then add strained juice and egg whites to mixture and whisk all together until white and frothy.

Chill and serve in small glasses.

Lemon pudding

cooking time: 40–45 minutes

you will need for 4 servings:

2 eggs, separated	1 oz. cornflour
6 oz. sugar	pinch salt
1 lemon	½ pint milk

1 Beat yolks with sugar and grated lemon rind.

2 Mix cornflour and salt smoothly with lemon juice and add to eggs and sugar.

3 Heat milk almost to boiling point, pour on to egg mixture and stir well.

4 Beat egg whites stiffly and fold into mixture.

5 Pour into buttered custard cups or individual fire-proof dishes. Stand in a baking tin of warm water and bake in a moderate oven (350°F.–Gas Mark 4) for 40–45 minutes. Serve cold.

Lemon snow

cooking time: few minutes

you will need for 4 servings:

¾ oz. gelatine	6 oz. sugar (4 oz. if fruit
4 tablespoons cold water	juice is used)
½ pint boiling water or	¼ pint lemon juice
juice from canned fruit	3 egg whites

1 Put gelatine with the cold water and leave to soak for a few minutes.
2 Add water or juice and sugar, stir over gentle heat until gelatine and sugar have dissolved.
3 Add lemon juice and leave to get cold then whisk till light and frothy.
4 Beat egg whites stiffly and fold into mixture.
5 Pour into a wetted mould and leave to set.

Lemon sponge

cooking time: 5 minutes

you will need for 4 servings:

2 lemons	2 egg whites
½ pint water	glacé cherries and
3 oz. sugar	angelica to decorate
½ oz. gelatine	

1 Pare lemons very thinly, then squeeze out juice. Put rind into a pan with water, sugar, gelatine and lemon juice.
2 Heat very slowly until sugar and gelatine melt. Remove from the heat, cover and leave to stand for 10 minutes.
3 Strain into a bowl and leave to get cold.
4 Add the egg whites and whisk all well together until the mixture is thick and spongy.
5 Pile into a serving dish and decorate with glacé cherries and angelica.

Meringues

cooking time: 3–4 hours

you will need for 4 servings:

4 egg whites	8 oz. castor sugar
pinch of salt	oil

1 If possible allow egg whites to stand overnight before making the meringues.
2 Add salt and beat the whites until they stand up firmly.
3 Sift in 4 oz. sugar and beat until stiff and dry.
4 Sift in remaining sugar and fold in, using a metal spoon.
5 Cover a board or heavy baking sheet with greaseproof paper and brush lightly with oil.
6 Shape meringues with two dessertspoons or use a bag and pipe.
7 Dry off in a very cool oven (225°F. – Gas Mark ¼) for 3–4 hours.

8 Leave to get quite cold before storing in an airtight tin.

Variations

Nut meringues – add 4 oz. chopped walnuts or hazel nuts to the basic meringue mixture and dry off as instructed. When quite cold, put pairs together with whipped cream and roll in chopped nuts.

Tutti-fruitti meringues – fill meringues with whipped cream to which has been added:
2 oz. glacé cherries, finely chopped.
2 oz. crystallised fruit, finely chopped.

Ginger meringues – fill meringues with whipped cream to which has been added 2 oz. chopped crystallised ginger.

Orange omelette

cooking time: 3–4 minutes

you will need for 4 servings:

1 orange	1–2 oz. hazel nuts, finely
3 eggs	chopped
pinch salt	1½ oz. butter
1 teaspoon sugar	castor sugar
1 teaspoon cream	

1 Grate orange rind.
2 Beat eggs, grated orange rind, salt, sugar and cream.
3 Remove all the pith from the orange and cut flesh into small pieces. Mix with the finely chopped hazel nuts.
4 Heat butter in an omelette pan, pour in egg mixture and stir lightly with a fork.
5 When the omelette begins to set, loosen edges with a palette knife.
6 When lightly set, place the orange mixture in the centre and fold the omelette over.
Serve at once, sprinkled with castor sugar.

Orange and lemon charlotte

cooking time: few minutes

you will need for 4 servings:

boudoir biscuits or	juice of 3 lemons
sponge fingers	1 small can mandarin
apricot jam or marmalade	oranges
3 eggs	1 tablespoon gelatine
6 oz. sugar	¼ pint thick cream

1 Halve biscuits lengthwise, spread sugary side lightly with jam and arrange round a charlotte mould or small round cake tin, putting the flat side against the mould.
2 Separate eggs and put yolks into a bowl with the sugar, lemon juice and syrup from the mandarins,

reserving 2 tablespoons to melt the gelatine.

3 Whisk over a pan of hot water until mixture is thick and creamy.

4 Remove from heat, add dissolved gelatine and leave until mixture is cold and beginning to set.

5 Fold in lightly whipped cream, stiffly beaten egg whites and some of the mandarin slices, cut into small pieces.

6 Spoon into prepared mould and leave to set.

7 Turn out and decorate with remaining mandarin sections.

Note:

This is a suitable sweet for a picnic and can be made in a round or square plastic picnic box. When lining the box be sure the biscuits do not stand up above the edge, so that the lid can be put on easily for transport. The remaining mandarins can be carried in another container.

Orange flummery

cooking time: few minutes

you will need for 4 servings:

2 oranges	1 pint orange jelly tablet
1 tablespoon cornflour	2–3 oz. sugar
¼ pint water	2 egg whites

1 Grate rind from 1 orange and put into a pan with juice from both oranges.

2 Mix cornflour smoothly with a little of the cold water, add remaining water and then add to orange juice and orange jelly tablet.

3 Add sugar and stir till boiling, boil for 1 minute.

4 Leave to get cold, then beat well and fold in stiffly beaten whites. Serve in individual glasses.

Omelette soufflé

cooking time: 6–7 minutes

you will need for 4 servings:

4 eggs	½ oz. butter
1 dessertspoon sugar	2 tablespoons hot jam
2 tablespoons cream or top of milk	castor sugar

1 Separate eggs, beat yolks with sugar and cream until mixture is creamy.

2 Beat egg whites stiffly, add egg yolk mixture and fold it into whites, using a 'cutting' action, until well blended.

3 In a strong pan (about 8-inches diameter) heat butter and when it is frothy, pour in egg mixture.

4 Leave for 1–2 minutes till underside is brown and then finish under the grill or put into a moderately hot oven (335°F. – Gas Mark 3) for 3–4 minutes.

5 Spread with hot jam and fold over.

6 Slide out on to a hot dish and sprinkle with castor sugar. Serve at once.

Variations

Banana omelette soufflé – omit the jam. Slice 2 bananas and fry lightly in butter. Sprinkle with castor sugar and 1 tablespoon rum. Arrange on half the omelette, fold over and finish as before.

With icing sugar – for a professional finish, use icing sugar. Sprinkle it liberally over the omelette and then make a lattice pattern across the top with a red hot skewer.

Queen of puddings

cooking time: about 1 hour

you will need for 4 servings:

½ pint milk	1½ oz. castor sugar
2 oz. cake crumbs or breadcrumbs	2 eggs
¼ oz. butter	1 tablespoon jam or jelly

1 Heat milk and pour over the crumbs.

2 Add butter and ½ oz. sugar and leave for about ½ hour.

3 Beat 1 whole egg and 1 egg yolk and stir into milk and breadcrumbs, then pour into a buttered pie dish.

4 Bake about ½ hour in a moderate oven (350°F. – Gas Mark 4).

5 When set, spread carefully with jam or jelly.

6 Beat remaining egg white till frothy. Add remaining sugar and beat till stiff.

7 Pile on top of the pudding and return to a slow oven (300°F. – Gas Mark 2) for about ½ hour or until the meringue is lightly coloured.

Savoy pudding

cooking time: 1¼ hours

you will need for 4 servings:

8 oz. stale Savoy or sponge cake	2 oz. melted butter
2 oz. finely chopped mixed peel	1 wine glass sherry (optional)
½ pint milk	4½ oz. castor sugar
	3 eggs

1 Put the cake through a sieve. Add the mixed peel, milk, butter, sherry if used, and 1½ oz. of the sugar.

2 Separate the whites from the yolks of the eggs and add the yolks to the cake mixture. Beat thoroughly and pour the mixture into a buttered pie dish.

3 Bake in a moderate oven (350°F. – Gas Mark 4) for about 45 minutes until set.

4 Whisk the whites until stiff.

5 Lightly fold in the remaining sugar and pile the meringue over the pudding.

Bake in a very cool oven until the meringue is set and golden brown – about 30 minutes.

Strawberry honeycomb

cooking time: 10 minutes

you will need for 4 servings:
1 strawberry jelly	¼ pint milk
2 eggs	biscuits

Dissolve the jelly in ¼ pint hot water.
Separate the yolks and whites of the eggs. Beat the yolks.
Warm the milk and pour on to the yolks, stirring. Pour into a pan, previously rinsed in cold water, cook over a gentle heat until thick, stirring throughout.
Remove from heat and pour into a large bowl.
Stir the jelly into the milk mixture.
Whisk the whites until stiff, lightly fold into the jelly.
Pour into a 1½ pint mould and leave until set.
Turn out on to a plate and serve with crisp biscuits.

St. Clement's delight

cooking time: few minutes

you will need for 4 servings:
2 eggs	½ lemon
4 oz. castor sugar	
½ orange	sponge fingers

Separate eggs, put yolks with 2 oz. sugar, grated rind and juice of orange and lemon.
Stir over a pan of hot water until mixture thickens. Remove from heat and cool a little.
Beat egg whites till frothy, add remaining sugar and beat till stiff.
Fold into custard mixture and pour into small glasses. Chill well and serve with sponge fingers.

Pineapple jelly cream

cooking time: about 10 minutes

you will need for 4 servings:
1 pint packet pineapple jelly	½ pint milk
	1 egg
½ pint hot water	1 tablespoon sugar

Dissolve jelly in hot water and set aside to get quite cold but not set.
Warm milk, add to beaten egg, return to pan, add sugar and stir over very gentle heat until custard thickens. Leave to get cold.
When jelly and custard are both cold, gradually stir jelly into the custard. Pour into small wetted moulds and leave to set.

Prune whip

cooking time: 15–20 minutes

you will need for 4 servings:
4 oz. prunes	2 tablespoons sugar
strip lemon peel	
2 egg whites	cream

1 Put well washed prunes with lemon peel and a little water. Cook till tender, then rub through a sieve.
2 Beat egg whites stiffly, beat in sugar, add prune purée.
3 Turn into a small fireproof dish, stand it in a dish of warm water and bake in a very moderate oven (325°F. – Gas Mark 3) for about 15 minutes. Serve with cream.

Raspberry meringue pudding

cooking time: 30–40 minutes

you will need for 4 servings:
1 can raspberries	5 oz. castor sugar
2 individual sponge cakes	½ pint milk
2 eggs	

1 Drain the raspberries, reserving the juice, and place in the bottom of an ovenproof dish.
2 Cut the sponge cakes through lengthways and place over the raspberries.
3 Separate the yolks from the whites of the eggs.
4 Beat the yolks with 1 oz. of the sugar. Heat the milk and pour on to the yolks, stirring continuously.
5 Return to the pan (rinsed out in cold water) and cook over a gentle heat, stirring until the custard thickens. Pour over the sponge.
6 Whisk the egg whites until stiff, fold in 2 oz. sugar and whisk again until thick. Fold in the remaining sugar.
7 Pile on top of the pudding and bake in a cool oven (225°F. – Gas Mark ¼) until the meringue is crisp.

To thicken the juice – thicken the juice with arrowroot and serve with the pudding. Allow 1 teaspoon arrowroot to ¼ pint juice.

Raspberry soufflé

cooking time: 25–30 minutes

you will need for 4 servings:
8 oz. ripe raspberries	¼ teacup cream
2 oz. cornflour	3 eggs
2 oz. castor sugar	2 oz. cake crumbs

1 Butter a soufflé dish.
2 Sieve the raspberries and mix with the cornflour and sugar, stirring until smooth.
3 Add the cream, the egg yolks and cake crumbs.
4 Whisk the egg whites until stiff and fold them into the mixture. *continued*

5 Turn the mixture into the prepared soufflé dish and bake in a moderately hot oven (375°F. – Gas Mark 5) until well risen and firm.

Rice meringue

cooking time: about 2 hours

you will need for 4 servings:

1½ oz. rice	2 eggs, separated
1 pint milk	3 tablespoons sugar
1 lemon	Jam

1 Wash rice and put into a double pan with milk and thinly pared lemon peel. Cook very gently until rice is soft and creamy (about 1½ hours).

2 Remove from heat, discard lemon peel and allow rice to cool a little.

3 Add lemon juice, egg yolks and 1 tablespoon sugar.

4 Put a layer of jam in the bottom of a fireproof dish and cover with rice mixture.

5 Whisk egg whites with a pinch of salt until frothy. Add remaining sugar and beat until very stiff.

6 Pile meringue on top of pudding, sprinkle with sugar and put into a very moderate oven (325°F. – Gas Mark 3) until the meringue is crisp and lightly browned.

Zabaglione

cooking time: 10–15 minutes

you will need for 4 servings:

5 egg yolks	2 oz. castor sugar
1 whole egg	¼ pint Marsala

1 Put the egg yolks, whole egg and castor sugar in the top of a double saucepan, or in a heatproof bowl over a pan of simmering water.

2 Whisk the mixture until pale yellow and fluffy.

3 Gradually add the Marsala, and continue whisking until the mixture becomes thick enough to hold its shape, about 10 minutes.

4 Spoon at once into individual glasses and serve warm, accompanied by sponge fingers.

Vanilla cream pudding

cooking time: 20–25 minutes

you will need for 4 servings:

1¼ oz. cornflour	3 eggs
1 oz. sugar	2 tablespoons cream
1 pint milk	2 tablespoons apricot Jam
1 teaspoon vanilla essence	

1 Mix cornflour and sugar smoothly with a little cold milk. Put the rest on to heat.

2 Add mixed cornflour, stir till boiling and boil for

3 minutes. Remove from heat and add vanilla essence.

3 Separate eggs, beat yolks with cream and stir into pudding.

4 Fold in stiffly beaten egg whites.

5 Spread jam over the bottom of a fireproof dish and pour in the pudding.

6 Bake about 20 minutes in a moderate oven (350°F. – Gas Mark 4).

Vienna pudding

cooking time: 1¼ hours

you will need for 4 servings:

2 oz. sugar	2 oz. cherries
2 tablespoons water	1 oz. currants
½ pint milk	¼ teaspoon vanilla essence
3 oz. bread, crusts removed	2 eggs
1½ oz. shredded suet	

1 Put sugar with 2 tablespoons water into a saucepan.

2 Stir until the sugar has dissolved and boil gently until the mixture turns dark brown.

3 Cool slightly, then slowly add the milk.

4 Heat gently until all the caramel has dissolved in the milk.

5 Pour this over the bread, adding all the other ingredients except the eggs. Allow to stand for 1 hour.

6 Stir in the well beaten eggs and pour the mixture into a greased basin.

7 Cover with a piece of greased paper and steam gently.

8 Allow to cool slightly before turning out.

Sponge fingers

cooking time: 15 minutes

you will need for about 20 fingers:

3 eggs	3 oz. flour
3 oz. castor sugar	pinch salt

1 Whisk eggs and sugar in a bowl over warm water, until thick and creamy.

2 Remove from heat and continue whisking until the mixture cools.

3 Fold in the flour, previously sieved with a pinch of salt.

4 Use a forcing bag with a ½ inch plain tube. Pipe 'finger' lengths of mixture on a greased and floured tray, leaving a good space between.

5 Dredge with castor sugar.

6 Bake in a moderate oven (350°F. – Gas Mark 4) for 5–7 minutes.

These sponge fingers accompany the Zabaglione dessert.

Uncooked desserts

Apple snow

you will need for 4 servings:

1 tablespoon lemon juice	2 egg whites
¼ pint sweetened apple purée	few drops pink food colouring (optional)

1 Add lemon juice to apple purée.
2 Beat egg whites stiffly and fold in.
3 Add a few drops of cochineal or carmine to give a very pale pink colour.
Serve in individual glasses.

Banana and ginger cream

you will need for 4 servings:

6 oz. full cream cheese	2 egg whites
2 tablespoons stiffly whipped cream	3 bananas
2¼ oz. castor sugar	3–4 ginger nuts, crushed

1 Rub cheese through a sieve or beat well with a fork.
2 Add cream and ¼ oz. sugar.
3 Beat egg whites stiffly, fold in remaining sugar and stir in cheese mixture.
4 Peel and slice bananas and fold in.
5 Pile into a serving dish or put into individual dishes, sprinkle with ginger nut crumbs and chill well before serving.

Brandy whip

you will need for 4 servings:

2 eggs, separated	1 tablespoon brandy*
2 tablespoons sugar	

*Sherry or white wine may be substituted

1 Put the yolks with the sugar and brandy.
2 Beat until creamy, then stand basin over a pan of hot water and stir until mixture thickens.
3 Remove from heat, cool a little, then fold in the stiffly beaten egg whites. Serve in small glasses.

Cheese and fruit cream

you will need for 4 servings:

6 oz. cream cheese	1 teaspoon lemon juice
¼ pint milk	1 teaspoon grated lemon rind
2 oz. sugar	
1 oz. sultanas	
1 oz. seedless raisins	sponge fingers
2 oz. nuts, grated or minced	

1 Mix cheese and milk and beat till creamy.
2 Add sugar, fruit and nuts.
3 Stir in lemon juice and lemon rind.
Serve in individual dishes with sponge fingers.

Chocolate and orange whip

you will need for 4 servings:

2 oz. bar chocolate	1 egg white
juice ½ orange	

1 Grate chocolate, put with orange juice and stir over hot water till chocolate has melted.
2 Remove from the heat and leave to cool.
3 Beat egg white stiffly and fold into cooled chocolate. Serve in small glasses.

Chocolate mousse, no. 1

you will need for 4 servings:

3 oz. chocolate	½ teaspoon coffee essence
3 eggs	
½ teaspoon vanilla essence	¼ pint thick cream
	1 tablespoon rum

1 Melt chocolate in a basin over a pan of hot water, taking care it does not get too hot.
2 Remove from heat and leave to cool.
3 Separate eggs, beat yolks lightly, then beat gradually into the melted chocolate.
4 Add vanilla and coffee essence, or, if preferred, add ¼ teaspoon instant coffee dissolved in 1 dessertspoon hot water.
5 Beat cream until fairly stiff, add rum, then fold into chocolate mixture.
6 Beat eggs whites stiffly and add to chocolate and cream mixture, folding in a little at a time. Pour into a dish or individual glasses and chill well before serving.

Chocolate mousse, no. 2

you will need for 4 servings:

2 oz. plain chocolate	2 eggs
few drops vanilla essence	

1 Grate chocolate and put in a basin over hot water. Stir till melted, but do not let chocolate get hot.
2 Add vanilla essence.
3 Separate eggs, beat yolks and add to chocolate.
4 Beat egg whites stiffly and fold into mixture. Serve in small glasses.

Chocolate snow

you will need for 4 servings:

2 egg whites	2 teaspoons chocolate powder
2 tablespoons sugar	few drops vanilla essence

1 Beat egg whites until stiff.
2 Mix sugar and chocolate powder and sift into egg whites. Fold in lightly.
3 Add vanilla essence. Serve at once in small glasses.

Chocolate whip

you will need for 4 servings:
2½ oz. plain chocolate
4 tablespoons strong black coffee
4 egg whites
2 oz. castor sugar
chocolate vermicelli for decorating

1 Grate chocolate, add coffee and dissolve over a pan of hot water.
2 When smooth and liquid, remove from heat and cool.
3 Beat egg whites stiffly and whisk in sugar.
4 Stir about 2 tablespoons of this meringue mixture into the chocolate and mix well, then gradually fold in the rest of the meringue.
5 Pile in small glasses and sprinkle with chocolate vermicelli.

Coffee mousse

you will need for 4 servings:
1½ oz. sugar
3 eggs
½ pint milk
1 tablespoon instant coffee
1 dessertspoon gelatine
2 dessertspoons water
2 oz. plain chocolate
¼ pint thick cream

1 Mix sugar with 1 whole egg and 2 egg yolks and beat till creamy.
2 Warm milk with instant coffee and pour over eggs.
3 Return to pan and stir over gentle heat until custard thickens.
4 Put gelatine into a small basin, add water and chocolate broken into small pieces.
5 Heat over hot water until gelatine and chocolate melt, then stir into custard and leave to cool.
6 When mixture begins to set, using a metal tablespoon, gently fold in remaining stiffly beaten egg whites.
7 Mix in well and lastly fold in lightly whipped cream.
8 Pour into a serving dish or individual dishes and leave to set. Decorate as liked.

Lemon cream fluff

you will need for 4 servings:
3 eggs
5 oz. sugar
3 lemons
½ oz. gelatine
3 tablespoons hot water
whipped cream for decorating

1 Separate eggs, whisk yolks and sugar till pale and creamy.
2 Add grated rind of 2 lemons and gradually stir in juice of 3 lemons. Whisk all together until mixture becomes quite thick.
3 Dissolve gelatine in water, cool a little, then stir into egg mixture.
4 Beat egg whites stiffly and fold into mixture when it is just beginning to set.

5 Turn the mixture into individual glasses.
6 Decorate with whipped cream.

Egg snow

you will need for 1 serving:
1 egg
1–2 teaspoons sugar
1 tablespoon milk
orange or lemon juice to taste

1 Separate egg and mix yolk with sugar.
2 Add milk and flavouring.
3 Beat egg white stiffly and fold in.

Pineapple sponge

you will need for 4 servings:
1 can chopped pineapple
water
1 oz. sugar
juice ½ lemon
½ oz. powdered gelatine
2 egg whites

1 Drain pineapple juice, measure the quantity and make it up to ½ pint with water.
2 Put liquid into a pan, add sugar, lemon juice and gelatine and stir till gelatine has melted. Leave to cool.
3 Beat egg whites stiffly, gradually whisk in the cool syrup and continue to whisk until mixture begins to set.
4 Fold in most of the pineapple.
5 Pile into glasses.
6 Decorate with remaining pineapple.

Pineapple chiffon pie

you will need for 4 servings:
1 pineapple or lemon jelly
¼ pint hot water
2 eggs
1 small can pineapple
1 teaspoon lemon juice
1 teaspoon finely grated lemon rind
2 tablespoons castor sugar
pinch salt
8–9 inch cooked flan case
desiccated coconut (optional)

1 Dissolve the jelly in the hot water and leave in a cool place.
2 Separate the yolks from the whites of the eggs.
3 Add the drained chopped pineapple to the egg yolks.
4 Add the lemon juice, rind and a tablespoon of sugar. Place the bowl over a pan of hot water and cook until the mixture thickens, stirring. Remove from the heat.
5 Add the jelly and leave until cold.
6 Whisk the egg whites together with the salt until stiff. Fold in the remaining tablespoon of sugar.
7 Fold the egg whites into the pineapple mixture and pour into the pastry case.
8 Sprinkle with coconut, if liked.

Orange snow

you will need for 4 servings:

1 orange jelly	2 tablespoons desiccated
2 eggs	coconut
2 oz. castor sugar	4 glacé cherries

1 Dissolve jelly in a little hot water. Make up to ¾ pint with cold water.
2 Separate yolks from whites of eggs.
3 Beat yolks with sugar until thick and creamy.
4 Gradually stir jelly into yolk mixture. Leave in a cold place until just beginning to set.
5 Whisk egg whites until stiff, fold into almost setting jelly.
6 Divide the mixture between 4 individual dishes.
7 Sprinkle with coconut and decorate each with a glacé cherry.

Orange whip

you will need for 4 servings:

	to decorate:
3 teaspoons gelatine	
¼ pint fresh orange juice	glacé cherries
2 tablespoons lemon juice	angelica
3 eggs, separated	chopped nuts
4 oz. sugar	

1 Dissolve gelatine in 1 tablespoon warm water.
2 Mix orange and lemon juice and make up to ½ pint with water.

3 Add dissolved gelatine, stir well and leave until it begins to get syrupy.
4 Whisk yolks and sugar till thick and creamy.
5 Add thickened fruit juice and whisk well.
6 Beat egg whites stiffly and fold into the mixture. Serve in individual glasses decorated with cherries, angelica and nuts.

Pineapple jelly whip

you will need for 4 servings:

1 can pineapple rings	pinch salt
½ oz. powdered gelatine	squeeze lemon juice
2 eggs, separated	glacé cherries and
2 oz. sugar	angelica

1 Drain pineapple, measure juice and make up to ½ pint with water.
2 Cut rings into small wedges and put into a glass dish reserving some for decoration.
3 Dissolve gelatine in hot pineapple juice. Cool.
4 Beat egg yolks and sugar till light and creamy. Add salt and lemon juice and stir in gelatine.
5 Beat egg whites stiffly, add the egg yolk mixture and fold in carefully.
6 Pour over the pineapple in the dish and when firm enough, decorate with remaining pineapple, the cherries and angelica.

Flans, tarts and pies

Sweet and savoury

Cheese and celery flan

cooking time: about 40 minutes

you will need for 4 servings:

8 oz. short crust pastry	salt, pepper, Cayenne
(see page 90)	pepper
2 oz. butter	½ oz. gelatine
2 oz. flour	⅛ pint water
1 pint milk	1 head celery
8 oz. grated Cheddar or	2 oz. prawns (optional)
Cheshire cheese	

1 Line an oblong baking tin (about 11 inches × 7 inches) with pastry and bake blind (see page 91) for 30 minutes in a moderately hot oven (400°F. – Gas Mark 6).
2 Make a sauce with butter, flour and milk.
3 Add cheese and seasonings.
4 Dissolve gelatine in hot water, stir into sauce.
5 Chop celery and add to sauce.
6 Pour sauce into pastry case and decorate with prawns. Leave to set.

Cheese and haddock pie

cooking time: about 30 minutes

you will need for 6 servings:

2 lb. potatoes	1½ oz. flour
1 lb. fresh fillet haddock	milk – about ⅜ pint
1 bay leaf	6 oz. grated cheese
6 peppercorns	salt, pepper
2½ oz. butter	2 tomatoes

1 Cook potatoes in boiling salted water till tender.
2 Poach fish carefully in salted water with bay leaf and peppercorns.
3 When fish is cooked, remove carefully, strain stock and reserve ¼ pint.
4 Skin and flake fish.
5 Make a sauce with 1½ oz. butter, flour, fish stock and ¼ pint milk. Season carefully, add fish and 4 oz. cheese.
6 When potatoes are cooked, drain and beat with remaining butter and milk. Season carefully.
7 Arrange potato in a border around a buttered fire-proof dish, using a pipe or spoon. *continued*

47

8 Pile fish in the centre and sprinkle with remaining cheese.

9 Peel and slice tomatoes and arrange around the edge. Brown under the grill.

Cheese flan

cooking time: 30–35 minutes

you will need for 4 servings:

6 oz. short crust pastry (see page 90)	2 eggs
6 oz. Emmenthal or Gruyère cheese	salt, pepper
½ oz. flour	pinch nutmeg
	⅜ pint milk

1 Line a 7-inch flan ring or pie plate with pastry.

2 Grate cheese, add flour, beaten eggs, seasonings and milk.

3 Pour into pastry case and bake about 35 minutes in a moderately hot oven (350°F. – Gas Mark 4). Serve hot.

Cheese and leek pie

cooking time: 30–35 minutes

you will need for 4 servings:

4–5 leeks	4 oz. grated cheese
6 oz. short crust pastry (see page 90)	2–3 tablespoons thin cream or top of the milk
salt, pepper	
1 teaspoon cornflour	egg or milk for glazing

1 Wash leeks and parboil in boiling salted water for 10 minutes. Drain and chop.

2 Line a 7-inch pie plate with pastry.

3 Arrange leeks in pastry case and sprinkle with seasoned cornflour.

4 Cover with cheese and pour cream on top.

5 Roll out pastry trimmings and cut into strips. Twist each strip and arrange in a lattice over the pie.

6 Brush strips and edge of the pie with beaten egg or milk and bake about 10 minutes in a hot oven (450°F. – Gas Mark 8), then reduce the heat (to 350°F. – Gas Mark 4) and cook a further 20–25 minutes.

Cheese and mushroom pie

cooking time: about 35 minutes

you will need for 4 servings:

6 oz. short crust pastry (see page 90)	½ pint milk
1½ oz. butter	4 oz. grated cheese
¾ oz. cornflour	4 oz. mushrooms
1 teaspoon curry powder	salt, pepper
	2 tomatoes

1 Line a 7-inch pie plate with pastry, prick the bottom and bake blind (see page 91) for 15–20 minutes in a moderately hot oven (400°F. – Gas Mark 6).

2 Melt 1 oz. butter, add cornflour and curry powder and mix well.

3 Add milk gradually, stir till boiling and boil for 2–3 minutes.

4 Add 3 oz. cheese and the mushrooms, chopped and sautéed for a few minutes in remaining butter.

5 Season carefully and pour into baked pastry case.

6 Sprinkle remaining cheese on top, arrange sliced tomatoes round the edge and brown under the grill.

Cheese and onion tart

cooking time: about 1 hour

you will need for 4 servings:

12 oz. onions	6–8 oz. grated cheese
4 oz. rashers of streaky bacon	freshly ground black pepper
8 oz. short crust pastry (see page 90)	milk, or egg and milk, to glaze

1 Peel onions and cook in boiling salted water about 15 minutes. Drain and chop.

2 Remove rind and chop bacon coarsely. Fry till crisp and pour off excess fat.

3 Line a pie plate with 4 oz. pastry, put in a layer of cheese, cover with half the onions and add bacon.

4 Sprinkle with another layer of cheese. Add remaining onions and cover with remaining cheese. Sprinkle with pepper, and press the filling down to the pastry.

5 Roll out remaining pastry for the lid.

6 Damp edges, put on the lid and press edges well together. Knock them up with the back of a knife and neaten.

7 Make a slit in the top of the pastry to allow the steam to escape, brush over with milk or egg and milk and bake in a moderately hot oven (400°F. – Mark 6) for about 1 hour.

Custard tart

cooking time: about 1 hour

you will need for 4 servings:

6 oz. short crust pastry (see page 90)	vanilla essence
2 eggs	1 small can evaporated milk
1 oz. castor sugar	grated nutmeg

1 Line a deep pie plate with pastry, pressing the pastry well against the bottom and sides of the plate.

2 Beat the eggs and sugar together in a bowl adding the vanilla essence.

3 Pour the milk into a measuring jug and make up to ¾ pint with water.

4 Heat the milk in a pan, pour on to the egg mixture, stirring carefully.

5 Pour the custard into the pastry case, sprinkle with grated nutmeg.

Bake in a very moderate oven (350°F. – Gas Mark 4) until custard is set.

Variations

Apricot custard tart – make as before, covering the base of the tart with dried apricots which have been soaked overnight and stewed in a little water.

Mincemeat custard tart – make as before, spreading pastry with mincemeat before filling with custard.

Coconut custard tart – make as before, spreading pastry with raspberry jam. Omit the nutmeg and sprinkle finished tart with toasted coconut.

Custard tartlets – make as before, lining deep patty tins with pastry. Bake for about 20 minutes when filled with custard.

Cheese and parsley flan

cooking time: 25–30 minutes

you will need for 4 servings:

1 oz. butter	1 7-inch lightly baked
1 small onion, peeled and	pastry case (see page
sliced thinly	91)
6 oz. Gruyère cheese	2 eggs
1 oz. grated Parmesan	½ pint milk
cheese	¼ pint cream
1½ tablespoons finely	salt, pepper
chopped parsley	pinch nutmeg

1 Heat butter and fry onion till transparent.
2 Cut Gruyère cheese into small cubes and mix with onion, Parmesan and parsley.
3 Put into pastry case.
4 Beat eggs, add milk, cream, seasoning and nutmeg and pour over cheese mixture.
5 Bake for 10 minutes in a moderately hot oven (400°F. – Gas Mark 6). Then reduce heat to (325°F. – Gas Mark 3) and cook a further 15–20 minutes, until custard is set.

Cream cheese and apple flan

cooking time: 15 minutes

you will need for 4 servings:

1½ lb. cooking apples	1 level dessertspoon
¼ pint water	sugar
2 oz. castor sugar	1 8-inch baked pastry
4 oz. cream cheese	case
¼ pint single cream	**for the glaze:**
¼ level teaspoon	3 level teaspoons
cinnamon	cornflour
	¼ pint apple juice
	a little cochineal

1 Peel, core and slice the apples. Poach in water with sugar until tender.
2 When cooked, drain well, saving the juice. Leave to cool.
3 Beat the cream cheese until smooth. Beat in the cream. Add cinnamon and sugar.
4 Spread over the bottom of the cooked pastry case.

5 Cover with apples, pour the glaze over. Leave in a cool place until the glaze sets.

To make the glaze

1 Blend the cornflour with a little of the liquid and put the rest of the liquid on to heat.
2 Pour on to the mixed cornflour. Return to the pan.
3 Bring to the boil and boil for 3 minutes stirring all the time. Colour a pale pink with the cochineal.

Cheese and pineapple flan

no cooking

you will need for 4 servings:

1 small can pineapple	4 oz. cottage cheese
pieces	1 lemon
¾ oz. gelatine	¼ pint thick cream
2 eggs	1 8-inch baked pastry
pinch salt	case
4 oz. sugar	glacé cherries
4 tablespoons warm milk	

1 Drain juice from pineapple.
2 Put gelatine into a basin, add about ⅛ pint pineapple juice and leave to soak for 5 minutes.
3 Chop or crush pineapple.
4 Separate eggs, beat yolks with pinch of salt and 2 oz. sugar and add warm milk.
5 Stir over hot water until custard thickens, then remove from heat.
6 Add gelatine, stir till dissolved and leave to cool.
7 Stir cheese with pineapple, grated lemon rind and lemon juice.
8 Beat egg whites stiffly and add remaining sugar gradually. Fold into custard. Lastly add lightly whipped cream.
9 Pile into pastry case and decorate with chopped cherries. Chill thoroughly before serving.

Savoury apple flan

cooking time: approx. 1 hour 20 minutes

you will need for 4 servings:

1 lb. cooking apples	¼ pint milk
2 medium onions,	salt, pepper
parboiled	2 firm tomatoes
4 oz. short crust pastry	castor sugar
4 oz. grated cheese	
2 eggs	

1 Peel, core and slice apples, chop onions. Simmer in a little water until tender. Allow to cool.
2 Line a deep 8-inch pie plate or flat tin with pastry. Pour apple onion mixture into pastry case. Cover with grated cheese.
3 Beat eggs, add milk and salt and pepper. Pour over filling.
4 Bake at 400°F. – Gas Mark 6 for about 30 minutes.
5 Slice tomatoes, arrange on top of flan, sprinkle lightly with castor sugar. *continued*

49

6 Cook for a further 14 minutes until filling is set and pastry is cooked through.

Variation

With **mushrooms** – mushrooms, sliced and cooked gently in butter or oil, may be used to garnish flan in place of tomatoes.

Cheese and potato pie

cooking time: about 30 minutes

you will need for 4 servings:

1½ lb. potatoes	6 oz. grated cheese,
2 oz. butter	Cheddar, Cheshire or
2 tablespoons top of the	Lancashire
milk	freshly ground black
	pepper
	2–3 tomatoes

1 Cook potatoes in boiling salted water.

2 Drain thoroughly, add butter and top of the milk and beat till light and fluffy.

3 Add most of the cheese, pepper, and extra salt if required.

4 Put into a buttered dish and arrange peeled and sliced tomatoes on top.

5 Sprinkle with remaining cheese and bake about 30 minutes in a fairly hot oven (400°F. – Gas Mark 6). Serve with salad or a green vegetable.

Cheese and raisin pie

cooking time: 35 minutes

you will need for 4 servings:

8 oz. short crust pastry	1 egg
(see page 90)	salt, pepper
½ oz. butter	pinch nutmeg
½ oz. flour	6 oz. seedless raisins
½ pint milk	extra milk
4½ oz. grated cheese	

1 Line an 8-inch pie plate with 4 oz. pastry.

2 Make a sauce with butter, flour and milk.

3 When cooled a little, add most of the cheese, beaten egg, seasonings, nutmeg and raisins.

4 Pour into pastry case, damp edges and cover with remaining pastry, pressing the edges well together.

5 Neaten the edge and make one or two slits in the top crust.

6 Brush over with milk and sprinkle with remaining cheese.

7 Bake in a moderately hot oven (400°F. – Gas Mark 6).

Note:

This pie is excellent served cold and makes a good picnic dish.

Cheese and shrimp pie

cooking time: 10 minutes

you will need for 4 servings:

6 eggs	1 oz. butter
½ pint cheese sauce (see	1 oz. grated cheese
page 91)	2 tablespoons bread-
1 4–oz. can shrimps	crumbs

1 Boil the eggs for 7 minutes, then put into cold water for 1 minute before removing the shells.

2 Chop the eggs roughly, and mix with the sauce.

3 Add the shrimps and butter and correct the seasoning.

4 Pour into a greased fireproof dish. Sprinkle with the cheese and breadcrumbs mixed together and brown in a hot oven or under the grill.

Golden cheese tarts

cooking time: 20–25 minutes

you will need for 4 servings:

4 oz. short crust pastry	2 oz. strong flavoured
(see page 90)	cheese, grated
2 oz. breadcrumbs	5 tablespoons milk and
1 level teaspoon baking	water
powder	½ level teaspoon salt
1 oz. margarine, melted	pinch pepper
1 beaten egg	good pinch mustard

1 Roll the pastry out thinly and use to line 10–12 patty tins.

2 Mix all the other ingredients together and place a spoonful in each pastry case.

3 Bake in a moderately hot oven (400°F. – Gas Mark 6) on the second shelf from the top.

4 Serve hot or cold with salad.

Cheese tart

cooking time: 45–50 minutes

you will need for 4 servings:

6 oz. short crust pastry	3–4 tablespoons cream
(see page 90)	6 oz. grated cheese
2 oz. butter	salt, pepper, Cayenne
2 oz. flour	pepper
¾ pint milk	pinch nutmeg
3 eggs	

1 Line a 7-inch pie plate with pastry. Prick the bottom and bake blind (see page 91) for 15 minutes in a moderately hot oven (400°F. – Gas Mark 6).

2 Make a white sauce with butter, flour and milk, remove from heat and cool a little.

3 Beat in eggs one at a time, stir in cream and cheese.

4 Season carefully and pour into the pastry case.

5 Bake for 30–35 minutes in a moderate oven (350°F. – Gas Mark 4).

Serve hot or cold with salad.

Cheese tartlets

cooking time: 15–20 minutes

you will need for 4 servings:

4 oz. short crust pastry (see page 90)	2 oz. grated cheese
1 egg	salt, pepper
¼ pint milk	pinch nutmeg

1 Roll pastry very thinly, cut into 3-inch rounds and line some patty tins, pressing the pastry well into them. Prick the bottoms lightly with a fork.
2 Beat egg slightly, add milk, cheese, seasoning and nutmeg.
3 Pour carefully into patty tins and bake in a moderately hot oven (400°F. – Gas Mark 6) for about 15–20 minutes until custard is set.

Cheese and vegetable flan

cooking time: about 45 minutes

you will need for 4 servings:

6 oz. short crust pastry (see page 90)	**for the sauce:**
	1 oz. butter
1 small packet frozen mixed vegetables	¾ oz. cornflour
	½ pint milk
2 tomatoes	2 oz. grated cheese
2 hard-boiled eggs	salt, pepper
	¼ teaspoon made mustard

1 Line a flan ring with pastry and bake blind (see page 91) for about 25 minutes in a hot oven (425°F. – Gas Mark 7).
2 Cook vegetables, drain and arrange in pastry case with peeled and sliced tomatoes and sliced eggs.
3 Make sauce in the usual way (see page 91). Add most of the grated cheese, salt, pepper and mustard.
4 Pour over vegetables, sprinkle remaining cheese on top and cook a further 20 minutes in a fairly hot oven (400°F. – Gas Mark 6).

Bacon and egg flan

cooking time: 40 minutes

you will need for 4 servings:

6 oz. short crust pastry (see page 90)	salt, pepper
	¼ teaspoon dried mustard
2 eggs	
6 rashers streaky bacon	1 small can evaporated milk
3 oz. cheese	
	2 tomatoes (optional)

1 Line an 8-inch pie plate with the pastry.
2 Beat the eggs. Remove the rind from the bacon and chop roughly. Add to the beaten eggs with the grated cheese, salt, pepper and mustard.
3 Stir in the milk and pour the mixture into the pastry-lined plate.
4 Bake on the centre shelf of a moderately hot oven (350°F. – Gas Mark 4).

5 When cooked and golden, remove from the oven and garnish with slices of tomato if liked.
6 Serve hot or cold.

Egg and bacon pie

cooking time: 25–30 minutes

you will need for 4 servings:

6 oz. short crust pastry (see page 90)	4 eggs
	salt, pepper
8 rashers bacon	little milk

1 Line a 7–8-inch pie plate with 3 oz. pastry.
2 Arrange bacon on pastry and break eggs on top. Season lightly.
3 Cover with remaining pastry, seal the edges and decorate as liked.
4 Brush top with milk and bake in a hot oven (400°F. – Gas Mark 6) for 10 minutes. Then reduce the heat to 350°F. – Gas Mark 4 and cook a further 15–20 minutes. Serve hot or cold.

Egg and prawn pie

cooking time: about 15 minutes

you will need for 4 servings:

6 eggs	seasoning
¼ pint cheese sauce (see page 91)	2 tablespoons grated cheese
4 oz. prawns, fresh, canned or frozen	2 tablespoons bread-crumbs
squeeze lemon juice	½ oz. butter
1 tablespoon cream	

1 Boil eggs for 6 minutes. Plunge into cold water for a few minutes, then shell carefully and chop the eggs roughly.
2 Make the sauce, add prawns, lemon juice and cream and correct seasoning.
3 Pour over eggs into a greased fireproof dish.
4 Mix cheese and breadcrumbs, sprinkle on top, dot with butter and brown in a moderately hot oven (400°F. – Gas Mark 6) for 10 minutes.

Egg and shrimp flan

cooking time: 15–20 minutes

you will need for 4 servings:

6 eggs	¼ pint white sauce (see page 91)
½ oz. butter	
1 teaspoon made mustard	1 7-inch baked flan case (see page 91)
4 oz. fresh or 1 packet frozen shrimps	
salt, pepper	1–2 tablespoons grated cheese
little parsley, chopped	

1 Boil eggs for 7 minutes, shell and slice carefully.
2 Heat butter, add mustard, shrimps, seasoning and parsley and sauté for a few minutes.
3 Add white sauce and eggs. *continued*

4 Pour into pastry case, sprinkle with cheese and brown under the grill.

Egg and vegetable pie

cooking time: 20–25 minutes

you will need for 4 servings:

1½ lb. spinach or 1 packet frozen spinach	2–3 spring onions or chives
1 oz. butter	salt, pepper
1 lb. cooked mixed vegetables, carrots, peas, beans, etc.	3 eggs
	3 tablespoons milk

1 Cook spinach, drain well, then chop and put into a buttered fireproof dish. Dot with a little butter and season carefully.
2 Arrange vegetables on top and sprinkle with chopped onion or chives and seasoning.
3 Separate eggs, beat yolks with milk and seasoning.
4 Beat whites stiffly and fold into yolks.
5 Pour over vegetables and bake about 20 minutes in a moderate oven (350°F. – Gas Mark 4).

Italian pie

cooking time: about 40 minutes

you will need for 4 servings:

4 oz. macaroni	2 hard-boiled eggs, chopped
1 oz. butter	2 oz. grated cheese
4 oz. mushrooms, sliced	salt, pepper
2 teaspoons minced or finely chopped onion	2 tomatoes
½ pint white sauce (see page 91)	

1 Break the macaroni into 1-inch lengths and cook in boiling salted water until just tender, then drain and put into a buttered fireproof dish.
2 Meanwhile, heat butter and sauté sliced mushrooms and onion until onion is cooked.
3 Add to sauce with chopped eggs and 1 oz. cheese. Season carefully.
4 Pour over macaroni, sprinkle with remaining cheese.
5 Peel and slice tomatoes and arrange round the edge of the dish.
6 Cook in moderately hot oven (400°F. – Gas Mark 6) for 10 minutes until tomatoes are cooked.

German cheese tart

cooking time: 30 minutes

you will need for 4 servings:

2 oz. cornflour	2 oz. currants and sultanas, mixed
¼ pint milk	salt, pepper
2 eggs	1 7-inch baked pastry case (see page 91)
3 oz. grated cheese	

1 Mix the cornflour smoothly with a little of the milk, then stir in the rest of the milk.

2 Add the beaten eggs, cheese and fruit. Season.
3 Pour into the pastry case and bake for about 25–30 minutes in a moderately hot oven (375°F. – Gas Mark 5).

Guernsey pie

cooking time: approx. 40 minutes

you will need for 4 servings:

8 oz. short crust pastry	freshly ground pepper
8 oz. onions, peeled and sliced	12 oz. tomatoes, peeled and sliced
1 oz. butter	6 oz. cheese, grated coarsely or thinly sliced
2 level tablespoons flour	milk
¼ level teaspoon mustard	

1 Roll out half the pastry and use to line a 9-inch pie plate.
2 Sauté the onions in butter, until soft. Add flour, mustard and pepper and cook for 3 minutes, stirring throughout.
3 Add tomatoes and allow to cook for a further 5 minutes, allow to cool.
4 Cover the base of the pastry case with half the cheese, top with tomato onion mixture. Finish off with remaining cheese.
5 Roll out the remaining pastry, use to cover pie. Knock up edges, brush with milk and make a hole in centre of the top to allow the steam to escape.
6 Bake at 400°F. – Gas Mark 6 for 30–40 minutes.

Leek and ham tart

cooking time: 1 hour 10 minutes

you will need for 4 servings:

for the pastry:	for the filling:
8 oz. plain flour	4 oz. cooked ham, chopped
pinch salt	1 packet leek soup
5 oz. softened butter	½ pint milk
	¼ pint thin cream
anchovy fillets for garnish	2 eggs
	1 oz. cheese, grated

To make the pastry case
1 Sieve flour and salt and rub butter in thoroughly.
2 Form mixture into a ball; chill for 30 minutes.
3 Place dough in a 9-inch pie plate, press out with fingertips until plate is completely lined.
4 Prick the bottom and sides well with a fork and bake blind in a hot oven (425°F. – Gas Mark 7) for 10 minutes.

To make the filling
1 Place ham in the bottom of the pastry case.
2 Mix leek soup smoothly with milk, cream and beaten eggs.
3 Pour over the ham, sprinkle cheese on top.

4 Bake in a slow oven (325°F. – Gas Mark 3) until filling is set – about 1 hour.

5 Garnish with anchovy fillets and serve.

Lobster quiche

cooking time: about 35 minutes

you will need for 4 servings:

1 8-inch flan case made with 6 oz. short crust pastry	2 eggs seasoning
4 oz. cooked lobster or 1 can lobster	½ pint double cream 1 oz. grated Parmesan cheese

1 Bake the flan case 'blind' and allow to cool.

2 Flake the lobster into the pastry case.

3 Whisk the eggs, season to taste with salt and pepper and stir in the cream.

4 Pour over the lobster and sprinkle with grated cheese.

5 Bake in a moderate oven (350°F. – Gas Mark 4) for 35 minutes until golden brown.

Marrow and cheese flan

cooking time: 15–20 minutes

you will need for 4 servings:

12 oz. cooked marrow	4 oz. grated cheese
1 8-inch baked flan case (see page 91)	1 egg, separated 2 tomatoes, peeled and sliced
salt, pepper nutmeg	bacon rolls for garnish
¼ pint white sauce (see page 91)	

1 Drain marrow well, cut into cubes and put into flan case. Sprinkle with seasoning and nutmeg.

2 Make white sauce, season carefully, add most of the cheese and egg yolk.

3 Beat egg white stiffly, fold into sauce, then pour over marrow.

4 Arrange tomato slices round the edge and sprinkle remaining cheese on top of the filling.

5 Put into a moderately hot oven (400°F. – Gas Mark 6) for about 15 minutes to brown.

6 Grill bacon rolls and arrange on top.

Quiche lorraine

cooking time: 45 minutes

you will need for 4 servings:

4 oz. bacon rashers	2 eggs
1 7-inch pastry case, baked blind (see page 91)	¼ pint thin cream salt, freshly ground black pepper
6 oz. Gruyère cheese	

1 Fry bacon lightly to remove excess fat, cut into pieces and arrange in pastry case.

2 Dice cheese and put with bacon.

3 Beat eggs, add cream and seasoning and pour over bacon and cheese.

4 Bake about 45 minutes in a very moderate oven (325°F. – Gas Mark 3).

Quick cheese pizza

cooking time: 25 minutes

you will need for 4 servings:

6 oz. short crust pastry (see page 90)	1 teaspoon chopped parsley
½ oz. butter 1 tablespoon chopped onion	pinch oregano salt, pepper 6 triangles Swiss Gruyère cheese
1 lb. tomatoes, peeled and chopped	

1 Line a 7-inch pie plate with pastry.

2 Melt butter, add onion and cook till tender.

3 Add tomatoes and cook for a few minutes.

4 Add herbs and seasoning.

5 Pour into pastry case and arrange cheese triangles on top.

6 Bake in a moderately hot oven (400°F. – Gas Mark 6) for about 25 minutes.

Savoury pie

cooking time: 20–25 minutes

you will need:

8 oz. rice	nutmeg
2 lb. spinach	8 oz. lean bacon
2 oz. butter	3 eggs
salt, pepper	4 oz. grated cheese

1 Cook rice in boiling salted water till tender, then drain well.

2 Cook spinach, drain very thoroughly and chop.

3 Heat 1 oz. butter in pan, add spinach, seasoning and pinch nutmeg. Toss for a few minutes, then add rice and chopped bacon. Sauté all together for 3–4 minutes.

4 Remove from heat, add beaten eggs and 2 oz. cheese.

5 Put into a fireproof dish, sprinkle with the rest of the cheese and dot with remaining butter.

6 Bake in a fairly hot oven till crisp and golden (375°F. – Gas Mark 5) – about 20 minutes.

Sweet corn and cheese flan

cooking time: 15–20 minutes

you will need for 4 servings:

8 oz. cottage cheese	salt, pepper
2 oz. grated Parmesan cheese	1 7-inch baked flan case (see page 91)
1 can sweet corn	2 tomatoes, peeled and sliced
¼ teaspoon paprika	

1 Mix cottage cheese, Parmesan and drained sweet corn. Then season carefully. *continued*

53

2 If mixture is a little stiff, add 2–3 tablespoons milk or any liquor from the corn.

3 Turn into pastry case and arrange tomato slices round the edge.

4 Put into a moderate oven (350°F. – Gas Mark 4) for about 15 minutes.

Tomato flan

cooking time: about 35 minutes

you will need for 4 servings:

4–6 oz. short crust pastry (see page 90)
4 oz. grated cheese
1 14-oz. can peeled tomatoes
2 beaten eggs
salt, pepper

1 level tablespoon very finely chopped onion (optional)
1 level teaspoon cornflour
chopped parsley (optional)

1 Roll out the pastry and use to line an 8-inch plain flan ring or sandwich tin.

2 Bake 'blind' in a moderately hot oven (400°F. – Gas Mark 6) for 15 minutes.

3 After 10 minutes, remove the baking beans and continue cooking for 5 minutes.

4 Place the pastry case on a baking tray.

5 Mix the cheese, tomatoes, eggs, seasoning, onion, if used, and the cornflour together.

6 Pour into the pastry case and bake in a very moderate oven (325°F. – Gas Mark 3) until the filling is just set.

7 Garnish with chopped parsley and serve hot or cold with watercress and buttered rolls.

Vegetable potato pie

cooking time: 30 minutes

you will need for 4 servings:

1 lb. cooked mixed vegetables
3 hard-boiled eggs
salt, pepper
1 tablespoon chopped parsley
¾ pint cheese sauce (see page 91)

1 lb. cooked potatoes
2–3 tablespoons hot milk
½ oz. butter
extra milk
1 tablespoon grated cheese

1 Dice vegetables and put into a buttered fireproof dish.

2 Slice eggs and arrange on top. Add seasoning and sprinkle with parsley.

3 Make cheese sauce and pour over vegetables.

4 Beat potatoes with hot milk and butter and correct the seasoning. Spread on top of the pie, ridge with a fork and brush with milk.

5 Sprinkle with cheese and bake about 30 minutes in a moderately hot oven (375°F. – Gas Mark 5).

Vegetable flan

cooking time: about 30 minutes

you will need for 4 servings:

6 oz. pastry
2–3 sticks celery, cooked
1 leek or onion, cooked
few green vegetables, cooked

1 carrot, cooked
2–3 oz. cheese, grated
1 egg
½ pint milk
salt, pepper

1 Line a flan ring with pastry.

2 Cut up the vegetables and place in the flan case. Sprinkle on half the cheese.

3 Beat up the egg, add the milk and season well.

4 Pour this mixture over the vegetables, sprinkle on the remaining cheese and bake in a moderate oven (350°F. – Gas Mark 4).

Variation

Using other vegetables – any suitable combination of cooked vegetables can be used in this way.

Vegetable pie

cooking time: 10–15 minutes

you will need for 4 servings:

1½–2 lb. cooked vegetables (carrots, onion, celery, etc.)
1 pint thin cheese sauce (see page 91)

1½ lb. cooked potatoes
2 oz. butter
1 small egg
salt, pepper

1 Arrange the vegetables and sauce in layers in an ovenproof dish, finishing with a layer of sauce.

2 Sieve the potato while hot, or mash thoroughly to remove any lumps.

3 Beat in the butter and the egg, saving enough egg for glazing, and seasoning.

4 Using a large star pipe, pipe the potato round the edge of the dish twice, to make a deep crust. Alternatively, spread the potato over the top of the dish and mark with the back of a fork.

5 Brush with remaining egg and brown in a moderately hot oven (400°F. – Gas Mark 6) for 10–15 minutes.

Spinach flan

cooking time: 40–50 minutes

you will need for 4 servings:

6 oz. flan pastry (see page 90)
1 lb. frozen spinach
2 eggs
½ pint milk

8 oz. cottage cheese
4 oz. grated Parmesan or Gruyère cheese
salt, pepper
nutmeg

1 Line an 8-inch pie plate with pastry and bake blind, for 10 minutes.

2 Cook spinach, according to the instructions on the packet and drain well.

3 Blend together eggs, milk, cottage and grated cheese. Add salt, pepper and nutmeg to taste.

4 Beat in the spinach.

5 Pour mixture into the flan case and bake at 350°F. – Gas Mark 4 for 30–40 minutes until the filling is set.

Dips and snacks

Cheese and anchovy crostini

cooking time: 8–10 minutes

you will need for 4 servings:

1 French loaf	1 can anchovy fillets
Bel Paese cheese	4 oz. butter

1 Cut bread into ¼-inch thick rounds and put a slice of cheese on each.

2 Arrange in a baking dish overlapping each other and put into a moderately hot oven (400°F. – Gas Mark 6) until the cheese has melted and the bread is crisp.

3 Mash anchovy fillets and put with the butter. Mix well, heat slightly, then spread over the bread.

Cheese beignets

cooking time: about 5 minutes

you will need:

	for the batter:
8 oz. Cheddar cheese	2 oz. flour
fat for frying	pinch salt
	1 egg
	about ¼ pint milk

1 Cut cheese into 1½–2-inch cubes.

2 Sift flour and salt, make a well in the centre and add egg and a little milk. Beat till smooth.

3 Add sufficient extra milk to make a fairly thick batter and beat thoroughly.

4 Dip the pieces of cheese in batter and fry in hot deep fat.

5 Drain well. Serve with a green salad.

Cheese dip

no cooking

you will need:

¼ small red pepper	1 teaspoon capers
4–6 stuffed olives	8 oz. cottage cheese
2–3 gherkins	salt, Cayenne pepper

1 Slice red pepper very thinly, slice olives.

2 Chop gherkins and capers.

3 Mix all ingredients together, season carefully and leave to stand for 1 hour before use.
Serve as a dip with crisp bread, biscuits or potato crisps, or use as a filling for rolls.

Cheese and bacon savoury

cooking time: 10 minutes

you will need for 4 servings:

8 oz. grated cheese	salt, Cayenne pepper
1 egg	½ oz. butter
1 teaspoon Worcester-	4 rounds bread
shire sauce	4 rashers bacon
¼ teaspoon made mustard	4 black olives

1 Mix cheese with beaten egg, seasonings and butter.

2 Spread mixture on the bread and put bacon rashers on top.

3 Cook for 10 minutes in a fairly hot oven (400°F. – Gas Mark 6).

4 Garnish each with an olive and serve hot.

Cheese balls

cooking time: 5–6 minutes

you will need for 2 servings:

4 oz. grated cheese	salt, Cayenne pepper
2 oz. flour	fat for frying
2 eggs, separated	

1 Mix cheese, flour and beaten egg yolks.

2 Add seasoning.

3 Beat egg whites stiffly and fold into mixture.

4 Fry in spoonfuls in deep fat, until well risen and golden brown. Serve with green salad.

Cheese and fish rolls

cooking time: few minutes

you will need for 4 servings:

1 small can tuna fish or	salt, pepper
salmon	4 large round bread rolls
1 small can or 1 packet	butter
frozen peas	4 slices cheese
1 small can evaporated	
milk	

1 Flake fish and add to peas, milk and seasoning.

2 Stir over gentle heat till mixture is smooth and creamy.

3 Split rolls, spread with butter and put a slice of cheese on one half of each roll. Pile some of the hot fish mixture on top and cover with the other half of roll. Serve at once with salad.

Cheese and ham savoury

cooking time: 5 minutes

you will need for 4 servings:

4 slices cooked ham	4 slices Gruyère cheese
4 rounds buttered toast	2 tomatoes
little chutney	

1 Put a slice of ham on each piece of toast.
2 Spread lightly with chutney and cover with cheese.
3 Peel and slice tomatoes and arrange on top.
4 Put under the grill to heat through.

Cheese ramekins

cooking time: 10 minutes

you will need for 4 servings:

2 rashers streaky bacon	freshly ground black
¼ pint thin cream	pepper
1½ oz. Gruyère cheese	Cayenne pepper
1½ oz. Parmesan cheese	2 eggs, separated

1 Butter 4 ramekin dishes or individual soufflé dishes.
2 Grill bacon till crisp, then crumble.
3 Heat cream, add grated cheeses and stir till melted.
4 Remove from heat, add black pepper, pinch Cayenne pepper and bacon.
5 Mix in egg yolks and fold in stiffly beaten egg whites.
6 Put into prepared dishes and bake in a hot oven (425°F.–Gas Mark 7) for 10 minutes.

Cheese rarebit puff

cooking time: 7–10 minutes

you will need for 4 servings:

4 rounds toast	¼ teaspoon made mustard
butter	salt, pepper
3 eggs	1 tablespoon cream
4 oz. grated cheese	

1 Make the toast, spread with butter and arrange the slices in a fireproof dish.
2 Separate eggs. Beat yolks with cheese, mustard, seasoning and cream.
3 Beat egg whites stiffly and fold into mixture.
4 Pile mixture on to toast and put into a moderately hot oven (400°F.–Gas Mark 6) until brown on top.

Cheese scotch eggs

cooking time: 3–4 minutes

you will need:

6 oz. grated cheese	1 egg
1½ oz. flour	1–2 tablespoons milk
salt, pepper	4 hard-boiled eggs
1 teaspoon Worcester-	breadcrumbs
shire sauce	fat for frying

1 Mix cheese, flour, seasoning and sauce.
2 Beat egg and add to cheese mixture with enough milk to bind.

3 Flour eggs lightly, then, with wet hands, coat eggs with cheese mixture.
4 Roll in breadcrumbs and deep fry in hot fat till golden brown.
5 Drain well. Serve cold with salad.

Cheese slices

cooking time: 20 minutes

you will need:

6 oz. Cheddar cheese,	Cayenne pepper
finely grated	1 egg
1½ oz. butter	8 oz. flaky pastry (see
salt, pepper	page 90)

1 Mix cheese with butter, add salt, pepper and a dash of Cayenne pepper.
2 Add beaten egg and mix well.
3 Roll pastry to about ¼-inch in thickness, halve and trim the edges.
4 Put one piece of pastry on to a wetted baking tin, and spread the filling on top.
5 Moisten edges and cover with remaining pastry. Press well to seal the edges, then knock them up with the back of a knife.
6 Mark into 12 equal portions, brush over with milk and bake for 20 minutes in a fairly hot oven (400°F.–Gas Mark 6).

Cheese toast

cooking time: 3–4 minutes

you will need for 2 servings:

1 oz. butter	salt, pepper
⅜ oz. flour	little French mustard
1½ gills creamy milk	2 rounds buttered toast
2 oz. grated cheese	

1 Melt butter, add flour and mix well.
2 Add milk and stir till boiling. Boil for 1 minute.
3 Remove from heat, stir in cheese and seasonings.
4 Pour over the toast and brown under the grill.

Cheese and bacon snack

cooking time: 20 minutes

you will need for 4 servings:

8 bridge rolls	2 oz. Cheddar cheese,
butter	grated
4 rashers streaky bacon,	2 tablespoons chutney or
grilled	sweet pickle

1 Split rolls and butter each side.
2 Cut rashers in half. Place one piece of bacon on the bottom half of each roll.
3 Blend the cheese and chutney together to form a paste. Spread on to the buttered side of each half of roll.

4 Press halves together and wrap each in foil. Heat in a moderate oven (350°F. – Gas Mark 4) for 15 minutes. Serve at once.

Variation

With mustard – a little made mustard may be used instead of chutney. If necessary, moisten cheese with 'top of the milk' to a spreading consistency.

Cheese and tomato dip

cooking time: 5–7 minutes

you will need:

1 oz. butter	3 eggs
8 oz. Cheddar cheese, grated	salt, pepper
$\frac{1}{4}$ pint tomato juice	pinch basil or oregano

1 Melt butter, add cheese and stir over gentle heat until melted.

2 Add tomato juice and lightly beaten eggs and cook slowly till mixture begins to thicken.

3 Remove from heat, add seasoning and herbs. Serve with biscuits or crispbread, or as a sandwich spread.

Garlic cheese

you will need for 4 servings:

2 cloves garlic, finely chopped	2 tablespoons top of the milk
8 oz. cream cheese	1 tablespoon parsley, finely chopped

1 Beat the garlic into the cream cheese, adding the milk, to make a dipping consistency.

2 Stir in the parsley.

3 Serve in a bowl, with hotel biscuits or celery sticks for dipping.

Variation

Lazy garlic cheese – if preferred use Lazy Garlic. Puff the Lazy Garlic into the cheese to taste. Add chopped chives or spring onions instead of parsley.

Cheese and tomato toast

cooking time: 6–8 minutes

you will need for 1 sandwich:

3 rounds bread	little made mustard
butter	2 tomatoes, peeled and sliced
4 oz. grated cheese	salt, pepper
1 tablespoon milk	

1 Toast each round of bread on one side and butter the untoasted sides.

2 Beat cheese to a paste with milk and mustard and spread on the buttered sides of toast.

3 Arrange tomato slices on top, sprinkle with salt and pepper and put under the grill until cheese begins to sizzle.

4 Assemble the sandwich by putting the slices on top of each other, cheese side uppermost. Press lightly together and cut into triangles.

Cream cheese with peppers

no cooking

you will need:

8 oz. cream or cottage cheese	1 dessertspoon finely chopped onion
1 dessertspoon tomato purée	$\frac{1}{2}$ small green pepper
	$\frac{1}{2}$ small red pepper
	seasoning as required

1 Mix the cheese, tomato purée and onion together.

2 Remove the seeds from the peppers and chop very finely. Add to the cheese and add a little salt if necessary. Chill.

3 Use as a dip or a filling for rolls and sandwiches.

Cream cheese and watercress dip

no cooking

you will need:

8 oz. cream cheese	1 oz. walnuts, chopped
salad cream	paprika
1 bunch watercress	chives
3–4 stuffed olives, sliced	

1 Mix cream cheese with sufficient salad cream to soften.

2 Wash and dry watercress, chop roughly and add to cheese, with olives and walnuts. Correct seasoning.

3 Pile into a serving dish and sprinkle with paprika and chopped chives.

Party dip

you will need:

1 ($1\frac{1}{2}$ pint) packet leek soup	2 oz. cheese, finely grated
2 (5 fl. oz.) cartons soured cream	1 tablespoon chopped walnuts
	paprika pepper

1 Stir the dry soup mix into the soured cream, mix well, adding the grated cheese.

2 Leave in the refrigerator overnight.

3 Sprinkle chopped nuts on the surface and dust with paprika.

4 Serve with small biscuits or celery and carrot sticks.

Variation

Celery party dip – make and serve as before, using packet celery soup. Omit walnuts and sprinkle with chopped chives.

Note: It is important that these dips are kept in the refrigerator until served.

Egg and anchovy toast

no cooking

you will need for 1 serving:
2 hard-boiled eggs
mayonnaise or salad
  cream (see page 89)
salt, pepper
1 round buttered toast
fillets of anchovy

1 Chop eggs coarsely and bind with mayonnaise or salad cream.
2 Add seasoning as required and pile on toast.
3 Criss-cross with fillets of anchovy.

Egg canapés

cooking time: about 5 minutes

you will need for 1 serving:
1 thin slice lean cooked
  ham
1 round hot buttered
  toast
1 slice Gruyère cheese
1 egg
salt, pepper

1 Put ham on toast and cover with cheese.
2 Separate egg and beat white stiffly with a little salt and pepper.
3 Spread egg white over cheese, make a hollow in the centre and drop in the yolk.
4 Put into a fairly hot oven (400°F. – Gas Mark 6) until the yolk is set.

Egg rolls

cooking time: 6–7 minutes

you will need for 4 servings:
4 large crusty rolls
4 eggs
salt, pepper
½ oz. butter
2 oz. grated cheese

1 Cut the tops from rolls and remove the centres.
2 Carefully break an egg into each roll.
3 Sprinkle with salt and pepper, add a small nut of butter and sprinkle with cheese.
4 Bake in a moderately hot oven (400°F. – Gas Mark 6) until eggs are set – about 6 minutes.

Eggs in tomato nests

cooking time: 10–12 minutes

you will need for 4 servings:
4 large firm tomatoes
salt, pepper
butter or oil for frying
4 slices bread
4 thin slices ham
4 eggs

1 Wipe tomatoes and cut a slice from each stalk end.
2 Remove seeds carefully, sprinkle insides of the tomatoes with salt and pepper and turn upside down. Leave for about 15 minutes to drain.
3 Put the tomatoes into a pan with about 1 tablespoon oil or butter, cover and cook very gently for about 5 minutes.

4 Fry bread lightly but not crisply.
5 Arrange a slice of ham on each piece of bread and stand a tomato on top.
6 Break eggs carefully into tomato cases, sprinkle with salt and pepper and put into a fairly hot oven (400°F. – Gas Mark 6) for 5–6 minutes.

Fried cheese fingers

cooking time: 1–2 minutes

you will need for 4 servings:
4 ½-inch thick rounds
  bread
4 oz. Lancashire cheese,
  grated
1 oz. flour
1 teaspoon salt
pinch Cayenne pepper
½ teaspoon Worcester-
  shire sauce
1 egg
3 dessertspoons milk
fat for deep frying

1 Cut each round of bread into 3 fingers.
2 Mix the cheese, flour, seasoning and sauce.
3 Beat egg, add milk and mix with cheese mixture.
4 Spread thickly on the bread.
5 Deep fry in hot fat, placing cheese side down. Turn over, then drain. Serve at once.

Potato and cheese soup

cooking time: 20–30 minutes

you will need for 4 servings:
1½ lb. potatoes
salt, pepper
2 pints stock
½ oz. flour or cornflour
¼ pint milk
2 tablepoons chopped
  parsley
2–3 tablespoons finely
  grated cheese

1 Thinly slice the potatoes and cook in seasoned stock until soft.
2 Mash with a fork and stir in the flour blended with the milk.
3 Season and bring to the boil, adding more milk if required.
4 Mix the parsley and cheese together and sprinkle over the soup before serving.

Golden buck

cooking time: 8–10 minutes

you will need for 2 servings:
½ oz. butter
3 oz. grated cheese
2 tablespoons beer
¼ teaspoon Worcester-
  shire sauce
½ teaspoon lemon juice
pinch salt, Cayenne
  pepper
pinch celery salt
2 eggs
2 slices buttered toast

1 Melt the butter, add cheese, beer, sauce, juice and seasonings. Stir till smooth and creamy.
2 Beat eggs and stir into mixture.
3 Heat gently until thickened, then pour on to the toast.

Chicken broth with eggs and cheese

cooking time: 6 minutes

you will need for 4–6 servings:

2 eggs	2 teaspoons freshly
2 tablespoons freshly	chopped parsley
grated Parmesan	grated nutmeg
cheese	1½ pints chicken stock

1 Beat the eggs in a small jug, until just blended. Add the cheese, parsley and a sprinkle of nutmeg.
2 Bring the chicken stock to the boil in a heavy pan over a high heat.
3 Pour in the egg mixture, stirring all the time. Reduce heat, and allow the stock to simmer for 2–3 minutes.
4 Adjust seasoning, pour into individual soup bowls and serve at once.

Note: The egg mixture will form white 'threads' or 'flakes' in the stock.

Ham and cheese balls

cooking time: 3–4 minutes for frying

you will need:

1 oz. butter	2 oz. grated cheese
1 oz. flour	salt, pepper
¼ pint milk	little made mustard
2 oz. breadcrumbs	egg and breadcrumbs for
1 hard-boiled egg, finely	coating
chopped	deep fat for frying
4 oz. chopped cooked	
ham	

1 Make a thick panada (see page 91) with the butter, flour and milk.
2 Add breadcrumbs, egg, ham, cheese and seasoning and mix all well together.
3 Shape into balls and coat with egg and breadcrumbs.
4 Fry in deep fat till brown and crisp.
Serve hot or cold with salad.

White foam soup

cooking time: 20–30 minutes

you will need for 4 servings:

1½ oz. butter	pinch ground mace
1 oz. plain flour	salt, pepper
2 pints milk	2 eggs
1 onion, chopped	4 oz. cheese, grated
1 diced stick celery or	1 tablespoon chopped
1 teaspoon celery salt	parsley

1 Melt the butter, add the flour and cook for 1 minute, stirring continuously.
2 Gradually add the milk and bring to the boil, stirring all the time.
3 Add the onion, celery or celery salt, mace and seasoning and simmer until the vegetables are tender.
4 Remove from the heat and cool slightly.

5 Separate the yolks from the whites of eggs.
6 Add the cheese and the beaten egg yolks to the soup.
7 Reheat without boiling until the cheese melts.
8 Beat the egg whites until stiff and fold half into the soup.
9 Place the remaining egg white in a soup bowl, and pour the soup over.
10 Sprinkle with chopped parsley and serve at once.

Ham and cheeseburgers

cooking time: about 10 minutes

you will need for 4 servings:

8 oz. cooked ham	1 egg yolk, beaten
4 oz. sausage meat	8 small thin slices cheese
1 small onion, peeled and	egg and breadcrumbs for
minced	coating
pinch mixed herbs	deep fat for frying

1 Mince or chop the ham finely and mix with sausage meat, onion and herbs. Bind with yolk.
2 Divide into 8 portions, divide each portion in half and shape into two flat rounds with floured hands.
3 Sandwich each pair of rounds with a slice of cheese and press into a neat shape.
4 Coat each 'sandwich' with beaten egg and breadcrumbs and fry in deep fat.

Note: Do not make the fat too hot, as time must be allowed for the sausage meat to cook through.

Ham and cheese toasted sandwich

cooking time: 5 minutes

you will need for 1 serving:

2 rounds bread	little mustard
butter	1 slice cheese
1 slice ham	

1 Butter one side of each round of bread.
2 Put ham on one slice and spread lightly with mustard. Put cheese on top and cover with the second slice of bread, buttered side downwards.
3 Press together and toast on both sides.

Ham rarebit

cooking time: 5 minutes

you will need for 4 servings:

4 rounds bread	6 oz. Danish Blue cheese
butter	black pepper
4 slices ham	4 tablespoons bread-
mustard (optional)	crumbs

1 Spread bread thinly with butter.
2 Cover each round with a slice of ham and add a little mustard.
3 Spread a quarter of the cheese on each slice of ham.
4 Sprinkle with a little pepper and cover with bread-crumbs. *continued*

5 Dot with butter and cook under the grill until golden brown.

Ham toast

cooking time: 5–6 minutes

you will need for 4 servings:

6 oz. cooked ham	½ teaspoon made mustard
4 eggs	little milk or stock
salt, pepper	4 rounds buttered toast

1 Mince ham.
2 Beat eggs, add ham, seasoning and 3–4 tablespoons milk or stock.
3 Put all into a saucepan and stir over gentle heat until egg are cooked. Serve on hot buttered toast.

Ham and tomato cheese dip

no cooking

you will need:

6 oz. Wensleydale or cream cheese	1 stick celery
2 tablespoons cream	3 oz. chopped ham
2 tablespoons tomato purée	1 gherkin, chopped
	salt, pepper, Cayenne pepper

1 Break cheese with a fork, add cream and tomato purée and beat till soft and smooth.
2 Add all other ingredients and season carefully.

Italian rarebit

cooking time: about 10 minutes

you will need for 4 servings:

2 oz. butter	3 eggs
1 small onion, peeled and chopped	salt, pepper, pinch garlic salt
8 oz. tomatoes, peeled and chopped	4 rounds buttered toast
8 oz. Cheddar cheese, grated	chopped parsley

1 Melt butter, add onion and cook till lightly coloured.
2 Add tomatoes and cook 3–4 minutes.
3 Add cheese and stir till melted.
4 Add lightly beaten eggs and seasoning.
5 Stir over gentle heat till mixture thickens, then pile on the toast. Sprinkle with parsley.

Kipper rarebit

cooking time: 5 minutes

you will need for 4 servings:

8 oz. cooked kipper	1 teaspoon chopped parsley
8 oz. grated cheese	
4 rounds buttered toast	squeeze lemon juice
1 oz. butter	

1 Remove any bones and flake kipper finely. Mix with cheese.

2 Pile on to toast and put under the grill for a few minutes.
3 Mix butter, parsley and lemon juice. Form into a neat square pat. Divide into four and place a piece on each round of toast.

Quick mushroom rarebit

cooking time: 5 minutes

you will need for 4 servings:

1 can condensed cream of mushroom soup	½ small green pepper, chopped
8 oz. grated cheese	salt, pepper
6 stuffed olives, sliced	4 rounds buttered toast

1 Put soup into the top of a double boiler or in a basin over hot water.
2 Add cheese and stir until it melts and the mixture is hot.
3 Add olives and green pepper and check seasoning. Pour over the hot toast.

Manhattan savoury

cooking time: 3–4 minutes

you will need for 1 serving:

2 oz. grated cheese	1 round bread, cut fairly thick
2 teaspoons Worcestershire sauce	1 tomato, peeled and sliced

1 Mix cheese and sauce until creamy.
2 Toast bread on one side and spread cheese on untoasted side.
3 Arrange tomato slices on top and put under the grill to heat through.

Pink dip

you will need:

1 dessertspoon salad cream	2 3-oz. packets cream cheese spread
1 tablespoon tomato ketchup	pinch salt
	potato crisps

1 Mix the salad cream and ketchup together.
2 Cream the cheese until smooth, gradually work in salad cream mixture.
3 Add the salt, mix thoroughly and turn into a serving dish. Serve with potato crisps.

Onion dip

you will need:

2 3-oz. packets cream cheese spread	1 teaspoon finely grated onion
2 tablespoons milk or cream	dash paprika pepper
1 tablespoon lemon juice	1 teaspoon anchovy essence (optional)
	potato crisps

1 Cream the cheese until smooth. Add lemon juice to

the milk or cream and gradually add to the creamed cheese.

2 Work in the onion and pepper and the anchovy essence if used. Mix thoroughly and turn into a serving dish. Serve with potato crisps.

Sardine crisps

cooking time: 10 minutes

you will need for 4 servings:

1 can sardines	$\frac{1}{4}$ teaspoon Worcester-
2 oz. grated cheese	shire sauce
1 oz. breadcrumbs	few drops vinegar
$\frac{1}{4}$ teaspoon made mustard	4 slices buttered toast

1 Drain the oil from sardines and reserve it.
2 Mix cheese, breadcrumbs, mustard, sauce and vinegar.
3 Add enough of the oil to make a fairly soft mixture.
4 Mash sardines and spread over the toast.
5 Cover with cheese mixture and brown under the grill.

Mock crab toast

cooking time: about 10 minutes

you will need for 2 servings:

2 oz. grated cheese	2 teaspoons made
3 teaspoons anchovy	mustard
essence	salt, Cayenne pepper
2 teaspoons vinegar	2 rounds buttered toast
	watercress

1 Mix cheese, anchovy essence, vinegar and mustard and stir till smooth.
2 Season lightly.
3 Spread on the toast and cook in a moderately hot oven (400°F. – Gas Mark 6) for 10 minutes.
4 Garnish with watercress.

Savoury toast

cooking time: about 10 minutes

you will need:

1 oz. butter	$\frac{1}{8}$ teaspoon made mustard
$\frac{1}{4}$ pint milk	$\frac{1}{8}$ teaspoon Worcester-
2 oz. fresh breadcrumbs	shire sauce
4 oz. grated cheese	4 rounds buttered toast
1 egg	4 small gherkins
salt	
pepper	

1 Heat butter, add milk and breadcrumbs and stir until mixture is quite hot.
2 Remove from heat, add cheese, beaten egg, seasoning and sauce.
3 Return to heat and cook till mixture is thick and creamy, stirring all the time.
4 Pile on to toast and garnish with thinly sliced gherkin.

Scotch woodcock

cooking time: 5–10 minutes

you will need for 2 servings:

2 rounds toast	1 tablespoon milk
1 oz. anchovy butter (see	salt, pepper
page 89) or anchovy	1 oz. butter
paste	4 anchovy fillets
2 eggs	1–2 teaspoons capers

1 Spread toast with anchovy butter and cut each piece into 4 fingers.
2 Beat eggs, add milk and seasonings.
3 Heat butter, add egg mixture and stir until it begins to thicken.
4 Remove from heat and continue stirring until mixture becomes firm.
5 Pile on strips of toast and garnish with anchovy fillets and capers.

Toasted cheese sandwich

cooking time: about 5 minutes

you will need for 4 servings:

for the sandwiches:	for the coating:
butter	2 eggs
8 rounds bread	4 tablespoons milk
6 oz. Lancashire cheese,	pinch salt
sliced	pinch sugar
made mustard	1$\frac{1}{2}$ oz. butter
	1 teaspoon oil

1 Butter bread, cover 4 rounds with cheese and spread lightly with mustard. Then complete the sandwiches.
2 Beat eggs, add milk, salt and sugar.
3 Dip each sandwich in egg mixture.
4 Heat butter and oil, and brown the sandwiches on both sides. Drain well. Serve hot.

Tuna and cheese toast

cooking time: few minutes

you will need for 4 servings:

1 small can tuna fillets	1 teaspoon chopped
salt, pepper	chives
lemon juice	4 rounds buttered toast
	4 slices cheese

1 Flake fish finely, add a little of the oil, seasoning and a squeeze lemon juice.
2 Mix in chives.
3 Spread on toast, cover with cheese and brown under the grill.

Welsh rarebit with apple

cooking time: 8–10 minutes

you will need for 2 servings:

1 tablespoon butter	salt, Cayenne pepper
3 oz. grated cheese	2 rounds buttered toast
1 tablespoon milk or beer	or crispbread
1 teaspoon made mustard	1 apple, sliced thinly

1 Heat butter, add cheese, milk or beer and seasoning.

continued

2 Stir over gentle heat until cheese has melted.

3 Cover toast or crispbread with apple slices and pour cheese mixture on top.

4 Brown under the grill. Serve at once.

Vegetable rarebit

cooking time: 10–15 minutes

you will need for 4 servings:

2 oz. butter	2 oz. diced cooked
1 onion, peeled and	vegetables
chopped	2 eggs
2 tomatoes, peeled and	salt, pepper
chopped	4 rounds buttered toast
6 oz. grated cheese	

1 Heat butter, add onion and tomato and cook till onion is soft.

2 Add cheese, vegetables and beaten eggs.

3 Cook over gentle heat until eggs are lightly set.

4 Add seasoning as required and pile on the toast.

Yorkshire rarebit

cooking time: about 10 minutes

you will need for 1 serving:

2 oz. Cheshire cheese	pepper
small nut butter	vinegar
1 tablespoon milk	1 round buttered toast
little made mustard	1 poached egg

1 Cut cheese into small pieces, add to butter and milk and stir over gentle heat until mixture becomes smooth and creamy.

2 Add a little mustard, pepper and a few drops of vinegar.

3 Pour on to hot toast and place egg on top.

4 Serve at once.

Supper savouries

Asparagus milanese

cooking time: 10–15 minutes

you will need for 4 servings:

1 bundle asparagus	4 tablespoons grated
4 eggs	Parmesan cheese
salt, pepper	

1 Prepare asparagus and cook in boiling salted water.

2 Drain and arrange in a buttered fireproof dish.

3 Beat eggs, add seasoning and pour over asparagus.

4 Sprinkle with cheese and put into a slow oven (300°F. – Gas Mark 2) until eggs have set – about 10 minutes.

Aubergines with rice and cheese

cooking time: 25 minutes

you will need for 4 servings:

2 aubergines	2 oz. grated cheese
1 shallot, finely chopped	2 oz. cooked rice
½ small clove garlic	salt, pepper

1 Wipe the aubergines. Cut in half lengthways and remove the pulp (do not peel). Sprinkle a little salt into the aubergine cases. Turn upside down and leave for 30 minutes. This is to remove excess water.

2 Put the pulp into a basin with the shallot, garlic, most of the cheese, rice, salt and pepper. Mix all well together.

3 Pile into the aubergine shells, sprinkle with the remaining cheese and bake in a moderate oven (350°F. – Gas Mark 4).

Egg and cheese fricassée (2)

cooking time: 15–20 minutes

you will need for 4 servings:

4 hard-boiled eggs	¼ level teaspoon grated
½ pint white sauce (see	nutmeg
page 91)	salt, pepper
1 tablespoon chopped	6 oz. grated cheese
parsley	1 tablespoon bread-
	crumbs

1 Slice the eggs and put into a fireproof dish.

2 Make the white sauce.

3 Add parsley, nutmeg, seasoning and about 4 oz. of the cheese.

4 Pour over the eggs.

5 Mix the rest of the cheese and the breadcrumbs together and sprinkle over the top.

6 Brown in a moderately hot oven (375°F. Gas Mark 5) or under the grill.

Baked eggs with beans

cooking time: 35 minutes

you will need for 4 servings:

1 lb. French beans or 1	salt, pepper
large packet frozen	pinch nutmeg
beans	4 hard-boiled eggs
1 oz. butter	2 tablespoons grated
1 tablespoon minced	cheese
onion	1 tablespoon bread-
1 oz. flour	crumbs
½ pint milk	

1 Prepare and cook beans, drain and put in a layer in

the bottom of a shallow buttered fireproof dish.

2 Heat butter, add onion and cook until it just begins to colour.
3 Add flour and mix well.
4 Add milk gradually, stir till boiling, and boil for 3 minutes. Add seasoning and nutmeg.
5 Fill dish with layers of sliced egg, sauce and finishing with sauce.
6 Mix cheese and breadcrumbs and sprinkle on top.
7 Bake in a very moderate oven (335°F. – Gas Mark 3) for 25 minutes.

Baked eggs with cream

cooking time: 10–15 minutes

you will need for 2 servings:

2 eggs	2 teaspoons dry white
1 tablespoon cream	wine
1 dessertspoon grated	¼ teaspoon made mustard
cheese	salt, pepper
2 teaspoons lemon juice	breadcrumbs
	butter

1 Break eggs into a buttered ramekin case or individual casseroles.
2 Mix cream, cheese, lemon juice, white wine and mustard. Season carefully and pour over the eggs.
3 Sprinkle with breadcrumbs, dot with butter and bake in a pan of hot water in a moderate oven (350°F. – Gas Mark 4), for 10–15 minutes.
4 Serve at once.

Belgian eggs

cooking time: about 10 minutes

you will need for 4 servings:

6 hard-boiled eggs	1 teaspoon chopped
2 oz. butter	parsley
salt, pepper	¼ pint thin cream
4 oz. shrimps or prawns	1–2 tablespoons grated
	cheese

1 Break eggs with a fork and mix in butter.
2 Add seasoning, shrimps and parsley.
3 Put into a buttered fireproof dish and cover with cream.
4 Sprinkle with cheese and put into a moderate oven (350°F. – Gas Mark 4) or under the grill to brown.

Sherried scramble

cooking time: 20 minutes

you will need for 4 servings:

4–6 slices toast	8 oz. grated cheese
4–6 cooked thin rashers	6 lightly beaten eggs
bacon (optional)	¼ teaspoon salt
4 oz. butter	3 tablespoons light sherry
¼ pint evaporated milk	or dry white wine

1 Cover the slices of toast with the bacon rashers if used. Keep hot.

2 Melt half the butter in the top of a double saucepan and blend in the milk.
3 Add the cheese and stir until nearly melted.
4 Add the eggs and salt and cook gently, stirring all the time until thick and creamy.
5 Lightly mix in the remaining butter and the sherry or wine.
6 Pile on to the prepared toast and serve at once.

Egg à la tripe

cooking time: about 10 minutes

you will need for 4 servings:

6 hard-boiled eggs	½ pint basic white sauce
3–4 medium sized onions	(see page 91)
2 tablespoons butter	salt, pepper

1 Cut the eggs into slices.
2 Peel and slice onions and sauté in the butter until soft and lightly coloured.
3 Make the white sauce, add salt and pepper.
4 Add the eggs and onions.
5 Pour into a serving dish and serve hot sprinkled with chopped parsley or a little red pepper.

Baked celery custard

cooking time: 1 hour

you will need for 4 servings:

1 1 lb. 3 oz. can celery	salt, pepper
hearts	2 oz. cheese, grated
1 pint milk	grated nutmeg
4 eggs	

1 Chop celery and drain well.
2 Warm the milk.
3 Beat the eggs together, adding salt and pepper. Pour in the milk, stirring all the time.
4 Stir in the grated cheese.
5 Put the celery into an ovenproof dish.
6 Pour the custard mixture over. Sprinkle with grated nutmeg and place the ovenproof dish in a baking tin containing hot water.
7 Cover loosely with foil. Bake at 350°F. – Gas Mark 4 for 1 hour, until just set.

Cauliflower supper savoury

cooking time: 15–20 minutes

you will need for 4 servings:

1 cauliflower	¼ pint cheese sauce (see
1 hard-boiled egg	page 91)
1 onion, peeled and	2 tablespoons grated
chopped	cheese
4 rashers bacon, cut into	1 tablespoon bread-
strips	crumbs
	½ oz. butter

1 Prepare cauliflower, divide into flowerets and cook

in boiling salted water till just tender (6–7 minutes). Drain and put into a buttered fireproof dish.

2 Slice egg and put with cauliflower.

3 Fry onion and bacon together until onion is soft and transparent, then sprinkle over cauliflower.

4 Make cheese sauce and pour over.

5 Mix the cheese and breadcrumbs together. Sprinkle on top of the sauce, dot with the butter and place into a moderately hot oven (400°F. – Gas Mark 6) for 15–20 minutes until crisp and brown.

Cheese and cabbage supper savoury

cooking time: 5–10 minutes to brown

you will need for 4 servings:

about 1 lb. white cabbage	few caraway seeds
¼ pint well-flavoured	(optional)
cheese sauce (see	2 oz. grated cheese
page 91)	toast

1 Shred cabbage and cook in boiling salted water.

2 Drain well and use ¼ pint liquid with ¼ pint milk to make cheese sauce.

3 Mix cabbage lightly with cheese sauce and add caraway seeds.

4 Put into a buttered casserole, sprinkle with cheese and brown under the grill.
Serve with fingers of buttered toast.

Cheese kedgeree

cooking time: about 10 minutes

you will need for 4 servings:

8 oz. cooked rice	1 tablespoon chopped
8 oz. cooked smoked	parsley
haddock	6 oz. grated cheese
1 oz. butter	seasoning
2 hard-boiled eggs	1 lemon

1 Add rice to fish, flaked and free from skin and bone, and butter.

2 Heat slowly, stirring, until mixture is quite hot.

3 Add 1 egg, sliced, parsley, cheese and seasoning.

4 Pile on to a serving dish and decorate with the remaining sliced egg. Serve with wedges of lemon.

Cheese and tomato bake

cooking time: about 1 hour

you will need for 4 servings:

2 Spanish onions	breadcrumbs
1½ oz. butter	2 oz. grated cheese
2 lb. firm tomatoes	dry mustard
salt, pepper and castor	
sugar	

1 Peel the onions, cover with boiling water, and allow to stand for ½ hour.

2 Drain well, cut into thin slices. Fry in melted butter until lightly browned.

3 Skin tomatoes and slice thickly. Arrange a layer of tomatoes in the bottom of a buttered pie dish.

4 Sprinkle lightly with salt, pepper and castor sugar. Top with a layer of fried onion and sprinkle thickly with breadcrumbs and grated cheese, adding a pinch of mustard, if liked.

5 Repeat the layers again, finishing with breadcrumbs and cheese. Dot with butter.

6 Bake in a moderately hot oven (375°F. – Gas Mark 5) for about 50 minutes. Serve as an accompaniment to poached eggs or fish.

Cheese macaroni and cauliflower bake

cooking time: about 30 minutes

you will need for 4 servings:

8 oz. cooked cauliflower	1½ oz. butter
salt, pepper	1½ oz. plain flour
4 oz. macaroni, cooked	¾ pint milk
2½ oz. grated cheese	1 egg

1 Break the cauliflower into sprigs and put a layer in the bottom of a greased casserole.

2 Season lightly, then cover with a layer of macaroni and cheese.

3 Repeat this, finishing with cheese.

4 Melt the butter, add the flour and a little seasoning.

5 Gradually add the milk and stir until boiling, cool slightly and add the egg.

6 Pour over the vegetables, and bake in a very moderate oven (325°F. – Gas Mark 3).

Variation

With tomatoes – if preferred, tomatoes can be used instead of cauliflower.

Cheese and potato roll

cooking time: about 40 minutes

you will need for 4 servings:

1¼ lb. potatoes	pinch nutmeg
1 oz. butter	1 tablespoon tomato
8 oz. grated cheese	ketchup
1 teaspoon made mustard	1–2 eggs
salt, pepper	breadcrumbs for coating

1 Cook potatoes, drain well, add butter and beat till light and fluffy.

2 Add cheese, seasonings and flavourings.

3 Add enough beaten egg to bind but do not make the mixture too soft.

4 Turn on to a floured board and shape into a roll.

5 Brush with remaining egg and roll in breadcrumbs.

6 Wrap loosely in foil or cover with greased paper and bake in a very slow oven (300°F. – Gas Mark 1) for about 40 minutes.
Serve hot with tomato sauce (see page 91).

Cheese and tomato savoury

cooking time: 25–30 minutes

you will need for 4 servings:

1 oz. butter	½ teaspoon chopped fresh
¾ oz. flour	basil or 1 teaspoon
¼ pint canned tomato	chopped parsley
juice	2 eggs
salt, Cayenne pepper	2 oz. grated cheese
½ teaspoon sugar	

1 Melt butter, add flour and mix well. Add tomato juice, stir till boiling, then boil for 3 minutes, stirring all the time.
2 Remove from heat, add seasoning, sugar and herb.
3 Separate eggs, beat yolks and add to sauce. Add cheese.
4 Beat egg whites stiffly and fold into mixture.
5 Pour into a buttered fireproof dish and bake in a moderate oven (350°F. – Gas Mark 4) for 25–30 minutes.

Tomatoes tratatoria

cooking time: 15 minutes

you will need for 4 servings:

8 firm medium sized	1 2-oz. can anchovy fillets
tomatoes	pepper
2–3 oz. fresh bread-	pinch of sugar
crumbs	2 thin slices bread
2 oz. Cheddar cheese,	olive or corn oil
grated	8 black olives

1 Slice a lid off the top of the tomatoes, hollow out the centres with a teaspoon.
2 Chop the pulp and mix with breadcrumbs and cheese.
3 Drain the anchovies, reserve 8 for garnishing, chop the remainder and add to cheese mixture.
4 Sprinkle the inside of each tomato case with pepper and sugar. Fill with cheese and breadcrumbs, etc.
5 Bake at 325°F. – Gas Mark 3 for 15 minutes.
6 Meanwhile, cut 8 small rounds out of the slices of bread. Fry in oil until crisp.
7 Serve each tomato on a croûte of bread, garnished with an anchovy fillet and an olive.

Eggs aurore

cooking time: about 25 minutes

you will need for 4 servings:

½ oz. butter	¼ pint thick white sauce
1 shallot, peeled and	(see page 91)
sliced	2 tablespoons cream
8 oz. tomatoes, chopped	4 eggs
salt, pepper	4 rounds fried bread
pinch sugar	paprika or parsley for
	garnish

1 Melt butter, add shallot and tomatoes and cook to a thick pulp. Put through a sieve and add seasoning and sugar.

2 Make white sauce, add tomato pulp and cream and adjust the seasoning.
3 Poach eggs and arrange each on a round of fried bread.
4 Coat with sauce and sprinkle with a little paprika or chopped parsley. Serve at once.

Eggs benedict

cooking time: 10 minutes

you will need for 4 servings:

for the sauce:	4 muffins or baps
1 oz. butter	butter
1 tablespoon cornflour	4 thick slices ham
½ pint milk	4 eggs, poached (see
2 oz. grated cheese	page 5)
salt, Cayenne pepper	parsley and sautéed
	mushrooms for garnish

To make the sauce

1 Melt butter, blend in cornflour.
2 Remove from heat and pour in milk.
3 Bring to the boil, stirring, and boil for 3 minutes, stirring.
4 Remove from heat.
5 Stir in cheese and seasoning.

To complete the dish

1 Toast muffins on both sides.
2 Spread with a little butter.
3 Place a slice of ham on each muffin and top with an egg.
4 Pour the cheese sauce over and garnish with sprigs of parsley and the sautéed mushrooms.

Eggs andaluth

cooking time: 20 minutes

you will need for 4 servings:

1 small green pepper	2 oz. Cheddar cheese
1 small onion	4 eggs
2 oz. butter	salt, pepper
1 thick slice white bread	

1 Remove seeds from pepper, and chop finely.
2 Chop the onion. Fry onion and pepper in 1½ oz. butter for 10 minutes without browning.
3 Grate bread to make 2 heaped tablespoons of bread-crumbs. Grate cheese and mix with breadcrumbs.
4 Grease the inside of 4 ovenproof dishes. Divide onion and pepper mixture between the four dishes. Break one egg into each. Sprinkle with cheese and breadcrumbs, salt and pepper.
5 Dot with butter.
6 Bake at 350°F. – Gas Mark 4 for 10–15 minutes until eggs are just set and top is golden brown. Serve immediately.

Egg and cheese crisp

cooking time: 15 minutes

you will need for 4 servings:

1 oz. butter	2 hard-boiled eggs,
1 oz. flour	chopped
½ pint milk	4–6 oz. cooked ham,
¼ teaspoon made mustard	chopped
salt, Cayenne pepper	1 teaspoon chopped
4 oz. grated cheese	parsley
	2 packets potato crisps

1 Make a sauce with butter, flour and milk.
2 Add seasoning and most of the cheese.
3 Add eggs, ham and parsley and pour into a buttered fireproof dish.
4 Mix remaining cheese with crisps and sprinkle on top.
5 Put into a moderate oven (350°F. – Gas Mark 4) to heat through.

Egg and cheese supper savoury

cooking time: 40–45 minutes

you will need for 4 servings:

4 oz. macaroni	6 oz. grated cheese
2 oz. butter	1 small packet frozen
2 oz. flour	peas (cooked) or 4 oz.
1 pint milk	cooked peas
salt, pepper	4–6 rashers lean bacon
4 hard-boiled eggs	

1 Break macaroni and cook in boiling salted water for 10–12 minutes. Drain well.
2 Make a white sauce with butter, flour and milk, boil for 3 minutes and season carefully.
3 Add chopped eggs, most of the cheese and the peas.
4 Pour into a buttered fireproof dish with the macaroni and cover with remaining cheese.
5 Roll bacon rashers and arrange on top.
6 Cook in a moderate oven (350°F. – Gas Mark 4) for about 30–35 minutes.

Poached eggs on cabbage

cooking time: 15–20 minutes

you will need for 4 servings:

1 medium-sized firm	salt, pepper
hearted cabbage	1–2 tablespoons tomato
¼ pint basic white sauce	purée
(see page 91)	4 eggs, poached

1 Remove the outer leaves of the cabbage, cut into quarters and remove the hard stalk. Wash well, then shred finely.
2 Cook in boiling salted water until tender, then drain thoroughly.
3 Make the white sauce, add seasoning and tomato purée.
4 Reheat the cabbage in the sauce. Put into a shallow serving dish and arrange the poached eggs on top.

Eggs flamenco

cooking time: about 25 minutes

you will need for 4 servings:

6 oz. rice	lemon juice
2 oz. butter	4 rashers bacon
4 small bananas	4 eggs
salt, freshly ground black	
pepper	

1 Cook rice in boiling salted water for about 12 minutes.
2 Melt butter, add peeled and sliced bananas and fry for a few minutes.
3 When rice is cooked, drain well, stir in bananas and add seasonings and a squeeze of lemon juice. Put into a serving dish and keep hot.
4 Cut bacon into pieces, fry for a few minutes till crisp, then sprinkle over the rice.
5 Fry eggs and arrange on top.

Egg and ham savoury

cooking time: about 20 minutes

you will need for 4 servings:

3 oz. macaroni	½ pint cheese sauce (see
4 eggs	page 91)
4 thin slices cooked ham	

1 Cook macaroni in boiling salted water. Drain and put into a buttered fireproof dish.
2 While macaroni is cooking, put eggs into boiling water and boil gently for 5 minutes. Put into cold water and leave for a few minutes, then shell very carefully.
3 Wrap each egg in a slice of ham and arrange on the macaroni.
4 Coat with cheese sauce, sprinkle a little more cheese on top and brown under the grill.

Quick egg rissoles

cooking time: 5–7 minutes

you will need for 4 servings:

4 hard-boiled eggs	salt, pepper
1 tablespoon flour	1 fresh egg
1 tablespoon finely	1–2 tablespoons thin
chopped parsley	cream or milk
2 tablespoons finely	breadcrumbs
chopped ham	fat for frying

1 Chop the hard-boiled eggs and mix with the flour parsley, ham and seasoning.
2 Bind with the egg and cream.
3 Shape into rissoles, dip in milk and coat with breadcrumbs.
4 Fry in shallow fat until crisp and golden, turning once.

Eggs in mustard sauce

cooking time: about 15 minutes

you will need for 4 servings:

1 oz. butter	salt, pepper
1 oz. flour	1 tablespoon thin cream
½ pint milk	6 hard-boiled eggs
2 teaspoons dry mustard	4 oz. grated cheese
2 teaspoons vinegar	

1 Make a sauce with butter, flour and milk.
2 Mix mustard smoothly with vinegar, add to sauce and season carefully. Add cream.
3 Slice eggs and put into a buttered fireproof dish.
4 Sprinkle with 2 oz. cheese, cover with sauce; top with remaining cheese. Brown under grill.

Egg and mushroom supper dish

cooking time: 30 minutes

you will need for 4 servings:

4–6 eggs	1 oz. butter
12 firm button	½ pint gravy or stock
mushrooms	salt, pepper
2 small onions	4 slices toast, unbuttered

1 Hard-boil the eggs.
2 Allow to become cold, shell and slice thinly.
3 Slice the mushrooms and finely slice the onions. Fry in butter over a gentle heat for 10 minutes.
4 Add the gravy or stock, bring to the boil and season to taste.
5 Reduce heat, add the eggs, and cook for further 10 minutes. Pile on toast and serve.

Shortcut soufflé

cooking time: 35 minutes

you will need for 4 servings:

1 (1½ pint packet) cheese	¼ pint milk
sauce mix	2 large eggs

1 Grease a 5-inch soufflé dish.
2 Make up the cheese sauce as directed on the packet, using only ¼ pint milk.
3 Remove from the heat.
4 Separate the eggs. Stir the yolks into the sauce.
5 Whisk the egg whites until stiff, fold into the sauce.
6 Bake in a moderately hot oven (375°F. – Gas Mark 5) for 30 minutes. Serve at once.

Eggs à la princesse

cooking time: 10 minutes

you will need for 2 servings:

2 rounds white bread	salt, pepper
1 oz. butter	2 tablespoons cream
2 eggs	

1 Stamp a round from each slice of bread with a

3-inch plain cutter. Remove centre with a smaller cutter, thus forming a ring of bread.
2 Heat butter and fry bread rings till golden brown. Drain well, then put into a buttered fireproof dish.
3 Break eggs carefully into bread rings. Season lightly and pour cream over.
4 Cover and bake in a moderate oven (350°F. -- Gas Mark 4) till eggs are set. Serve at once.

Eggs on risotto

cooking time: about 30 minutes

you will need for 4 servings:

2 oz. butter	pinch mixed herbs
1 small onion, peeled and chopped	salt, pepper
	3 oz. grated cheese
6 oz. rice	4 eggs
1¼ pints stock (can be made with 1 chicken or beef stock cube)	parsley sprigs

1 Melt butter, add onion and rice and cook till golden.
2 Add stock and herbs and cook till rice is tender and stock absorbed.
3 Season if necessary and add cheese, reserving about 1 tablespoonful.
4 Turn risotto into a serving dish and keep hot.
5 Poach eggs and arrange on top, then sprinkle with remaining cheese. Garnish with parsley sprigs.

Eggs in snow

cooking time: few minutes

you will need for 1 serving:

1 round bread	salt, pepper
butter	pinch nutmeg
1 egg	little grated cheese

1 Toast bread on one side, turn and toast the other side very lightly.
2 Butter lightly toasted side and keep hot.
3 Separate egg, add seasoning and nutmeg to white and beat till stiff.
4 Spread egg white over buttered toast and drop yolk in the centre.
5 Sprinkle with a little cheese and put under the grill till the egg yolk is set. Serve at once.

Chicken broth with poached eggs

cooking time: 10 minutes

you will need for 4 servings:

2 oz. butter	2 tablespoons freshly grated Parmesan cheese
4 slices bread (½-inch thick)	
4 eggs	1 heaped tablespoon chopped parsley
1 pint chicken stock	

1 Warm 4 individual soup bowls. *continued*

2 Melt the butter over a moderate heat.

3 Fry the bread for 4–5 minutes, turning frequently, until both sides are golden brown. Keep the bread hot.

4 Bring the stock to simmering point in a large shallow pan. Poach the eggs in the stock, for 3–5 minutes (depending on how firm you wish them to be).

5 Cut the bread into triangles and place in the bottom of the 4 soup bowls.

6 Lift the eggs out of the stock, using a perforated spoon. Place one egg in each bowl. Pour stock round each egg.

7 Sprinkle with cheese and parsley; serve at once.

Egg and sausage roll

cooking time: about 1 hour

you will need for 6 servings:

8 oz. short crust pastry (see page 90)	4 hard-boiled eggs beaten egg or milk to
1 lb. pork sausage meat	glaze

1 Roll pastry out thinly into an oblong 11 × 9 inches.

2 Flatten the sausage meat with floured hands into a piece 11 × 4 inches.

3 Place the sausage meat on the pastry, and place the eggs in a line along the centre. Fold the sausage meat over the eggs.

4 Brush the edge of the pastry with water, fold the pastry over the sausage meat, and press the edges of pastry together to seal.

5 Place the roll on a baking tray, brush with egg or milk. Make a diagonal cut in the pastry over each egg.

6 Bake in a hot oven (400°F. – Gas Mark 6) on third shelf from top for 30 minutes.

7 Reduce to moderately hot (375°F. – Gas Mark 5) for further 30 minutes. Serve hot or cold.

Egg and spaghetti scramble

cooking time: about 20 minutes

you will need for 4 servings:

4 oz. spaghetti	1½ oz. butter
3 eggs	cooked, creamed spinach
salt, pepper	paprika
4 tablespoons thin cream or evaporated milk	

1 Break spaghetti into short pieces and cook in boiling salted water till tender. Drain well.

2 Beat eggs, add seasoning, cream and spaghetti.

3 Heat butter, add egg and spaghetti mixture and scramble in the usual way.

4 Serve on a bed of creamed spinach and sprinkle with paprika.

Curried scrambled eggs

cooking time: 15 minutes

you will need for 4 servings:

1 small onion	salt
½ oz. butter	¼ pint milk
1 teaspoon curry powder	buttered toast
4 eggs	lemon juice

1 Chop the onion finely. Melt the butter and fry the onion over a gentle heat for 3 minutes.

2 Sprinkle in the curry powder, allow to cook for 5 minutes, stirring throughout.

3 Beat the eggs lightly, add a good pinch of salt and the milk.

4 Pour the mixture into the pan and continue cooking until the eggs are set.

5 Pile on to hot buttered toast. Sprinkle with lemon juice and serve at once.

Variation

With chutney – spread the unbuttered toast with a sweet chutney, before topping with eggs.

Eggs in tomato juice

cooking time: 15–20 minutes

you will need for 4 servings:

1 small can tomato juice	1 teaspoon chopped
4 eggs	parsley
salt, pepper	creamed potatoes
sugar	

1 Pour tomato juice into a buttered shallow fireproof dish.

2 Break in each egg carefully and add a little seasoning and a pinch of sugar.

3 Bake in a slow oven (300°F. – Gas Mark 2) until the eggs are firm.

4 Sprinkle with parsley and serve with potatoes.

Note: The tomato juice gives the egg a pale pinkish colour which pleases children and gives a fillip to jaded appetites.

Egg and tomato savoury

cooking time: about 25 minutes

you will need for 4 servings:

3 tablespoons oil	salt, pepper
1 medium-sized onion, peeled and sliced	pinch sugar
1 lb. tomatoes, peeled and sliced	1 teaspoon chopped basil or parsley
1 small clove garlic	4 thin slices ham
	4 eggs

1 Heat the oil, add onion and cook till golden.

2 Add tomatoes, crushed garlic, seasoning, sugar and basil.

3 Cook slowly until mixture is reduced to a pulp (about 15 minutes).

4 Arrange ham in the bottom of a casserole and pour tomato purée over.

5 Break the eggs on top, cover and cook for about 7–8 minutes in a moderate oven (350°F. – Gas Mark 4).

Rice florentine

cooking time: 30 minutes

you will need for 4 servings:

4 oz. long grain rice	4 eggs
½ pint water	½ packet cheese sauce
½ teaspoon salt	½ pint milk
2 oz. butter	nutmeg
1 packet (4 oz.) frozen spinach	

1 Put rice, water and salt into a saucepan. Bring to the boil, stir once. Cover tightly and simmer for 15 minutes.

2 When the rice is cooked, melt the butter, add the spinach and cooked rice. Allow to cook over a gentle heat for about 10 minutes, stirring occasionally so that mixture is well blended.

3 Meanwhile, poach 4 eggs.

4 Make up cheese sauce as directed on the packet using ½ pint milk.

5 Divide spinach rice mixture between 4 individual dishes. Top each with a poached egg.

6 Pour sauce over and sprinkle with grated nutmeg. Serve at once.

Fried stuffed peppers

cooking time: about 10 minutes

you will need for 4 servings:

4 medium-sized green peppers	few drops Tabasco
	salt, freshly ground black pepper
6 oz. Cheddar cheese	
6 oz. Port Salut or Bel Paese cheese	2 tablespoons cornflour
	2 eggs, separated
	deep fat for frying

1 Parboil peppers for 10 minutes.

2 Drain well, make a small opening in one side of each pepper. Scoop out seeds and pith.

3 Dice cheeses, sprinkle with Tabasco and add seasoning.

4 Fill peppers with cheese. Reshape and coat with some of the cornflour.

5 Mix remaining cornflour smoothly with egg yolks.

6 Beat egg whites stiffly, fold lightly into cornflour mixture.

7 Coat peppers with batter and fry in deep fat.

8 Drain well and serve at once.

Ham and asparagus rolls

cooking time: 15–20 minutes

you will need for 4 servings:

1 can asparagus spears	1 tablespoon grated cheese
4 good slices cooked ham	
½ pint cheese sauce (see page 91)	1 dessertspoon bread-crumbs
	½ oz. butter

1 Drain asparagus and divide into 4 bundles. Wrap each in a slice of ham and arrange in a buttered fireproof dish.

2 Make sauce and pour over the rolls.

3 Mix cheese and breadcrumbs and sprinkle on top.

4 Dot with butter and put into a moderate oven (350°F. – Gas Mark 4) for about 10 minutes to heat through. Serve hot, from the dish.

Grilled ham and cheese rolls

cooking time: 15 minutes

you will need for 4 servings:

8 slices ham	oil
French mustard	4 pineapple rings
8 slices processed cheese	4 slices buttered toast
	watercress

1 Spread slices of ham with a little mustard. Top each slice of ham with a slice of cheese.

2 Roll up like a Swiss roll and secure each with a cocktail stick.

3 Brush each with oil and grill until cheese begins to melt. Remove from grill pan and keep hot.

4 Drain pineapple rings, brush with oil and grill for 5 minutes.

5 Place 1 pineapple ring on each piece of toast, top each with two ham rolls and garnish with watercress.

Leeks au gratin

cooking time: 20–25 minutes

you will need for 4 servings:

7–8 leeks	½ level teaspoon made mustard
2 oz. butter	
2 oz. cornflour	lemon juice
½ pint milk	2 tablespoons bread-crumbs
4 oz. grated cheese, Gruyère or Cheddar	little butter
salt and black pepper	

1 Prepare and wash the leeks thoroughly then cook in boiling salted water until just tender. Drain and put into a greased fireproof dish.

2 Melt the butter, add the cornflour and mix well. Cook for a few minutes, then remove from the heat.

3 Add the milk gradually, return to the heat, stir until boiling and boil for 1 minute.

4 Add cheese and continue cooking until it has melted,

then season carefully with salt, pepper, mustard and a squeeze of lemon juice.

5 Pour the sauce over the leeks, sprinkle with the crumbs and dot with butter.

6 Bake in a moderate oven (350°F. – Gas Mark 4) until the top is golden brown.

Mushrooms and cheese

cooking time: 25 minutes

you will need for 4 servings:

1 lb. mushrooms	salt, pepper
1 lemon	4 oz. cream cheese

1 Put mushrooms into a buttered fireproof dish. Sprinkle with lemon juice and seasoning.

2 Dot with spoonfuls of cream cheese.

3 Cover and bake about 25 minutes in a moderate oven (350°F. – Gas Mark 4).
Serve with a green salad.

Eggs boulangère

cooking time: 15–20 minutes

you will need for 4 servings:

2–4 cold cooked potatoes	3 oz. grated cheese
1 oz. butter	4 eggs
salt, pepper	2 tablespoons thin cream
nutmeg	or top of milk

1 Slice the potatoes and fry in the butter until brown on both sides.

2 Put into a greased fireproof dish and season with salt, pepper and a pinch of nutmeg.

3 Sprinkle the cheese on top.

4 Break each egg carefully on top of the cheese, sprinkle with salt and pepper and cover with the cream or milk.

5 Bake about 10 minutes in a moderate oven (350°F. – Gas Mark 4).

Baked stuffed onions

cooking time: 30 minutes

you will need for 4 servings:

4 medium-sized onions	butter
2 tablespoons bread-	mashed potatoes
crumbs	½ pint white sauce (see
3 oz. grated cheese	page 91)
salt, pepper	

1 Peel the onions and parboil in boiling salted water.

2 Drain and cool a little, then remove some of the inside with a small teaspoon.

3 Chop the onion which has been removed and mix with the breadcrumbs and half the cheese. Season carefully.

4 Add a little of the white sauce to moisten if necessary.

5 Fill the onions with this mixture, sprinkle with the rest of the cheese and dot with butter.

6 Bake in a moderately hot oven (375°F. – Gas Mark 5).

7 Serve on a bed of hot mashed potato and serve the sauce separately.

Potatoes au gratin

cooking time: 40 minutes

you will need for 4 servings:

2 lb. potatoes	salt, pepper
2 oz. butter	1 egg, separated
1 oz. flour	4 oz. grated cheese
½ pint milk	pinch nutmeg

1 Parboil potatoes, drain and slice fairly thickly. Put into a buttered fireproof dish.

2 Make a sauce with 1 oz. butter, flour and milk.

3 Add seasoning, egg yolk, most of the cheese and nutmeg.

4 Beat egg white stiffly and fold into sauce. Pour over potatoes.

5 Sprinkle remaining cheese on top, dot with remaining butter and bake in a moderately hot oven (400°F. – Gas Mark 6) for 40 minutes.
Serve with salad.

Potato and cheese crisp

cooking time: 30–40 minutes

you will need for 4 servings:

1½ lb. potatoes	salt, pepper
¼ pint milk	pinch nutmeg
2 eggs	2 tablespoons bread-
2½ oz. butter	crumbs
3 oz. grated cheese	

1 Cook potatoes in boiling salted water, drain well.

2 Add milk, beaten eggs, about 2 oz. butter, 2 oz. cheese, seasoning and nutmeg and beat all well together.

3 Put the mixture into a buttered fireproof dish. Mix remaining cheese with breadcrumbs and sprinkle on top.

4 Dot with remaining butter and bake in a moderate oven (350°F. – Gas Mark 4) until crisp and brown.

Potato and egg supper savoury

cooking time: 20–25 minutes

you will need for 4 servings:

2 lb. potatoes	4 hard-boiled eggs, sliced
4 oz. cream cheese	salt, pepper
1 tablespoon finely	3–4 tablespoons milk
chopped chives	½ oz. butter
	parsley sprigs

1 Parboil potatoes, drain and slice.

2 Put a layer of potato into a buttered fireproof dish.

3 Mix cream cheese and chives and spread a thin layer over the potatoes. Cover with egg slices.

4 Continue in layers, season lightly and finish with a layer of potatoes.

5 Add milk, dot with butter and cook in a moderately hot oven (400°F. – Gas Mark 6) for about 20 minutes.

6 Serve hot, garnished with parsley sprigs.

Potato and cheese ring

cooking time: 20–25 minutes

you will need for 4 servings:

1½ lb. potatoes	browned breadcrumbs
1 egg yolk	1 packet frozen peas
1½ oz. butter	2 tomatoes
3–4 oz. grated cheese	4 oz. mushrooms
salt, pepper	parsley
nutmeg	

1 Cook potatoes, drain well, then beat in the egg yolk, small nut of butter and grated cheese. Add seasoning and a good pinch nutmeg.

2 Butter a ring mould and sprinkle with breadcrumbs. Press in the potato mixture and smooth the top.

3 Bake about 20 minutes in a moderate oven (350°F. – Gas Mark 4).

4 Meanwhile cook peas, peel and slice tomatoes fairly thick and sauté in remaining butter for a few minutes with mushrooms.

5 When the potato ring is cooked, turn on to a hot serving dish.

6 Pile peas in the centre and garnish with tomatoes, mushrooms and a few sprigs of parsley.

Potatoes dauphinoise

cooking time: 30 minutes

you will need for 4 servings:

1 clove garlic	scant teaspoon salt
2½ lb. firm waxy potatoes	pinch of pepper
6 oz. grated Gruyère	3 oz. butter
cheese	½ pint milk

1 Bruise the garlic and rub it round the inside of an oven dish, approximately 10 inches diameter, 2 inches deep. Grease the inside of the dish with melted butter.

2 Peel the potatoes, cut into ⅜ inch slices. Dry well. Spread half the slices in the bottom of the dish.

3 Cover with half the cheese, sprinkle with salt and freshly ground black pepper and dot with butter.

4 Cover with remaining potatoes, season and sprinkle with cheese, dot with remaining butter.

5 Pour the milk in, down the side of the dish. Bring to simmering point over a low heat.

6 Cook at the top of a hot oven (425°F. – Gas Mark 7)

for 20–25 minutes until the potatoes are tender, all the milk absorbed and the top golden brown. Serve at once.

Potato and leek scallop

cooking time: about 1½ hours

you will need for 4 servings:

1½ lb. potatoes	1 oz. butter
3–4 leeks	¾ pint well flavoured
4 rashers bacon	cheese sauce (see page
salt, pepper	91)

1 Peel potatoes and slice fairly thickly. Put into boiling salted water and cook gently for 5 minutes, then drain.

2 Prepare leeks carefully, then slice.

3 Chop bacon and fry until crisp.

4 Arrange potatoes and leeks in alternate layers in a buttered casserole. Sprinkle each layer with a little seasoning and crumbled bacon. Dot potato layers with butter.

5 Pour cheese sauce over.

6 Cover and cook about 1½ hours in a slow oven (300°F. – Gas Mark 2).

Variation

With cheese and breadcrumbs – if you prefer the dish browned, when cooked, sprinkle with a mixture of breadcrumbs and grated cheese and brown under the grill, or raise the casserole to the top of the oven and increase the heat.

Potato scramble

cooking time: 20–25 minutes

you will need for 4 servings:

1 lb. cooked potatoes	1 teaspoon cornflour
2 rounds bread	⅛ pint milk
1 large onion	salt, pepper
2–3 tablespoons oil	chopped parsley
3 eggs	

1 Cube potatoes, dice the bread, peel and chop the onion.

2 Heat 2 tablespoons oil, add onion and fry till lightly brown. Remove from pan.

3 Add the bread, fry till brown, remove and put with onion.

4 Add a little extra oil if necessary and fry potatoes. When brown, return bread and onion to pan.

5 Beat eggs, add cornflour, mixed smoothly with the milk, and seasoning.

6 Pour egg mixture over the contents of the pan and stir over gentle heat until egg is set.

7 Put into a hot serving dish and sprinkle with parsley.

Lentils with cheese sauce

cooking time: 1½ hours

you will need for 4 servings:

6 oz. lentils	½ pint thick white sauce
1 clove garlic	(see page 91)
salt, pepper	3–4 oz. Lancashire cheese
	grated nutmeg, optional

1 Steep lentils for 2–3 hours, then drain. Place in pan with sufficient water to cover. Add garlic.
2 Simmer until lentils are tender, about 1 hour. Add salt and pepper to taste.
3 Make white sauce.
4 Grate or crumble cheese.
5 Drain lentils and turn into a flameproof dish. Pour white sauce over, cover surface with cheese, and sprinkle with grated nutmeg, if liked.
6 Bake at 350°F. – Gas Mark 4 for 25 minutes. Brown under a hot grill and serve.

Rice and egg savoury

cooking time: 30–40 minutes

you will need for 4 servings:

2 oz. butter	1 oz. seedless raisins
2 shallots, peeled and	2 tablespoons tomato
chopped	sauce
4 oz. rice	4 eggs
1 pint stock	1 teaspoon chopped
salt, pepper	parsley
2 oz. grated cheese	paprika

1 Melt butter, add shallots and washed rice and stir over low heat for about 5 minutes.
2 Add stock, stir till boiling and cook until rice is tender and stock absorbed.
3 Add seasoning, most of the cheese, the raisins and tomato sauce.
4 Turn into a serving dish and keep hot.
5 Poach the eggs and arrange on top of the rice.
6 Sprinkle with remaining cheese and garnish with parsley and paprika.

Sausage scramble

cooking time: 10 minutes

you will need for 4 servings:

4 sausages	salt, pepper
4 eggs	¼ teaspoon made mustard
2 tablespoons water	4 rounds buttered toast

1 Skin sausages and cut into small pieces.
2 Put into a heated frying pan and cook gently until the fat begins to run, then increase the heat a little and fry till brown.
3 Pour off any surplus fat.
4 Beat eggs lightly, add water and seasonings.
5 Pour into the pan with the sausages and stir until eggs are lightly cooked.
6 Serve on buttered toast.

Savoury bake

cooking time: 45–50 minutes

you will need for 4 servings:

4 oz. fresh breadcrumbs	6 oz. bacon, chopped
½ pint milk	1 small onion, peeled
3 eggs, separated	and chopped finely
salt, pepper	8 oz. cooked vegetables
½ teaspoon dry mustard	(carrots, peas, beans,
6 oz. grated cheese	etc.)

1 Put breadcrumbs into a large basin, add milk and leave to stand about 15 minutes.
2 Stir in egg yolks and all the other ingredients, seasoning carefully.
3 Whip egg whites stiffly and fold into mixture.
4 Turn into a buttered fireproof dish and bake in a moderate oven (350°F. – Gas Mark 4) till well risen and golden brown.

Savoury baked eggs

cooking time: 25 minutes

you will need for 4 servings:

8 oz. potatoes	2 oz. grated Cheddar
¼ oz. butter	cheese
1–2 tablespoons milk	4 eggs
salt, pepper	

1 Cook potatoes in boiling salted water until tender.
2 Drain well and mash with butter and milk.
3 Add seasoning and cheese and spread evenly in a buttered fireproof dish.
4 Make four hollows with the bottom of a wetted tumbler and break one egg into each.
5 Sprinkle lightly with salt and pepper and cook in a moderate oven (350°F. – Gas Mark 4) until the eggs are set.

Savoy potatoes

cooking time: 40–50 minutes

you will need for 4 servings:

1½ lb. potatoes	1 small clove garlic
4 oz. Gruyère cheese	1 chicken stock cube
salt, pepper	¾ pint boiling water

1 Peel potatoes and cut into ¼-inch thick slices.
2 Slice cheese very thinly.
3 Arrange potatoes and cheese in layers in a buttered fireproof dish, sprinkling each layer with seasoning, and a little crushed garlic. Finish with a potato layer.
4 Dissolve stock cube in boiling water and pour into the dish. It should not quite cover the top layer of potato.
5 Cook in a moderately hot oven (350°F. – Gas Mark 4) for about 45 minutes when the potatoes should be tender and nearly all the stock absorbed.
6 If liked, garnish with chopped parsley.

Savoury custard (1)

cooking time: 30 minutes

you will need for 2 servings:

½ pint milk
1 egg, beaten
salt, pepper

2 tablespoons grated
  cheese

Warm milk and pour over egg.

Add seasoning and cheese.

Pour into a buttered pie dish and stand the dish in a shallow pan of warm water.

Bake about 30 minutes or until set, in a very moderate oven (325°F. – Gas Mark 3).

Savoury custard (2)

cooking time: 45–50 minutes

you will need for 4 servings:

1 pint milk
½ teaspoon salt
pepper to taste
¼ teaspoon paprika,
  optional

1 tablespoon unsalted
  butter
2 large eggs
nutmeg

Heat milk to almost boiling point, adding salt, pepper and paprika, if used, and butter.

Beat eggs until well blended, stir in the hot milk. Strain into a buttered ovenproof dish.

Sprinkle with grated nutmeg.

Place dish in a baking tin containing warm water. Bake in a moderate oven (350°F. – Gas Mark 4) until set, 45–50 minutes.

Variations

Cheese custard – stir 4 oz. grated Lancashire cheese into the milk, after straining.

Onion custard – finely slice or chop one medium Spanish onion into the bottom of the dish, before pouring in the custard.

Scrambled eggs pepperoni

cooking time: 15–20 minutes

you will need for 4 servings:

2 medium-sized red or
  green peppers
2 tablespoons oil
1 small onion, peeled
  and chopped finely

2 tomatoes, peeled and
  sliced
½ clove garlic
salt, pepper
3 eggs
4 rounds buttered toast

1 Wash and seed the red or green peppers and slice very thinly.

2 Heat oil, add peppers and onion and cook gently for about 10 minutes until peppers begin to soften.

3 Add tomatoes and crushed garlic and continue cooking for about 5 minutes until mixture is soft and mushy.

4 Add seasoning and stir in the beaten eggs.

5 Cook over gentle heat until eggs are set.

6 Serve on toast.

Scalloped eggs

cooking time: 10 minutes

you will need for 4 servings:

4 eggs
4 anchovies
1 tablespoon capers

½ pint white sauce (see
  page 91)
browned breadcrumbs
butter

1 Hard-boil the eggs, then shell, cut into slices while still hot and put into a buttered fireproof dish.

2 Chop anchovies and capers and add to white sauce.

3 Pour over eggs and sprinkle with breadcrumbs.

4 Dot with butter and put into a moderately hot oven (350°F. – Gas Mark 4) for 10 minutes.

5 Serve hot.

Scrambled eggs with sweet corn

cooking time: 3–4 minutes

you will need for 4 servings:

4 eggs
salt, pepper
3 tablespoons water
¾ oz. butter

1 small can sweet corn
4 rounds buttered toast
chopped parsley

1 Beat the eggs lightly with the salt and pepper and water.

2 Melt butter, add eggs and cook over gentle heat until eggs begin to thicken.

3 Drain corn to remove as much moisture as possible and stir into the eggs.

4 Cook a further 1–2 minutes and pile on to the buttered toast. Garnish with chopped parsley.

Variation

With shrimps – if a few shrimps are available, they make a very good addition.

Stuffed courgettes

cooking time: about 10 minutes

you will need for 4 servings:

8 courgettes
1 oz. butter
1 small onion, peeled and
  chopped
1 tablespoon flour
6 oz. cooked veal, minced

3 oz. grated cheese
1 teaspoon tomato purée
little stock
salt, pepper
1 tablespoon oil

1 Halve courgettes lengthwise. Put into boiling water and leave for 3 minutes.

2 Drain and put under running cold water till cool.

3 Heat butter and fry onion till it begins to colour.

4 Add flour and veal and continue cooking till well browned. *continued*

5 Add most of the cheese, the tomato purée and enough stock to make a fairly soft mixture. Add seasoning and cook for a few minutes longer.

6 Drain courgettes, remove seeds and fill cavities with stuffing.

7 Brush with oil, sprinkle with remaining cheese and put into a hot oven (450°F. – Gas Mark 8) to heat through. Serve hot.

Corn supper dish

cooking time: 30 minutes

you will need for 6 servings:

1 egg	1 teaspoon chives or
¼ pint milk	parsley, finely chopped
3 oz. breadcrumbs	salt, pepper
1 large can sweet corn	½ oz. butter
4 oz. grated cheese	

1 Beat egg lightly, add milk and 2 oz. of the breadcrumbs.

2 Stir into the corn, with half the cheese, the chives or parsley. Add salt and pepper to taste.

3 Turn into a greased pie dish.

4 Mix the remainder of the breadcrumbs and cheese together. Sprinkle over the corn. Dot the surface with butter.

5 Bake for 30 minutes in a moderate oven (350°F. – Gas Mark 4).

Variations

With mustard – if preferred, the chives or parsley may be omitted, and dry mustard, to taste, added.

Corn stuffed peppers – this mixture may be used to stuff peppers.
Cut stalk end off peppers. Place upright in baking dish. Fill with corn mixture. Pour ½ pint tomato juice or stock into the dish. Cover and bake in a moderate oven for 30 minutes.
Remove lid and cook for further 10 minutes.

Sweet corn fritters

cooking time: 7–10 minutes

you will need for 4 servings:

½ can sweet corn	fat for frying
2 oz. flour	1–2 tablespoons grated
2 eggs	cheese
¼ pint milk	paprika
salt, pepper	

1 Drain corn, break it a little and add flour.

2 Separate eggs, beat yolks, and add milk.

3 Mix corn smoothly with egg and milk and add seasoning.

4 Beat egg whites stiffly and fold into mixture.

5 Fry in spoonfuls in hot deep fat till well risen and golden brown.

6 Drain well and sprinkle with cheese and paprika before serving.

Sweet corn savoury

cooking time: 10–15 minutes

you will need for 4 servings:

1 can sweet corn	4 oz. grated cheese
milk	4 eggs
2 oz. butter	1 tablespoon bread-
1½ oz. flour	crumbs
salt, Cayenne pepper	

1 Drain corn, measure the liquid and make it up to ¾ pint with milk.

2 Make a sauce with 1½ oz. butter, flour and milk and corn liquor.

3 Add seasoning, 3 oz. cheese and corn.

4 Boil eggs for 5 minutes.

5 Put half the sauce mixture into a buttered fireproof dish. Shell the eggs and arrange on top. Cover with remaining sauce.

6 Mix remaining cheese with breadcrumbs and sprinkle on top.

7 Dot with remaining butter and brown under the grill.

Swiss eggs

cooking time: 10 minutes

you will need for 3 servings:

3 eggs	1 teaspoon chopped
salt, pepper	parsley
2 oz. grated cheese	¼ pint cream
	½ oz. butter

1 Break eggs carefully into a buttered fireproof dish. Sprinkle lightly with salt and pepper.

2 Add half the cheese and parsley.

3 Add a little seasoning to cream and pour over eggs.

4 Sprinkle with remaining cheese and parsley, dot with butter and put into a moderate oven (350°F. – Gas Mark 4) till eggs are set.

Tomatoes au gratin

cooking time: 15 minutes

you will need for 4 servings:

1 lb. tomatoes	1 teaspoon chopped fresh
1 oz. butter	basil or pinch oregano
salt, pepper	4 oz. grated cheese
sugar	2 oz. breadcrumbs
	parsley sprigs

1 Peel tomatoes and slice thinly.

2 Put half into a buttered fireproof dish, dot with ½ oz. butter, and sprinkle with a little seasoning, sugar and basil.

3 Mix cheese and breadcrumbs and sprinkle half on top.

Repeat with remaining ingredients.

Bake for about 15 minutes in a fairly hot oven (400°F. – Gas Mark 6).

Serve at once, garnished with parsley sprigs.

Tomato macaroni cheese

cooking time: about 20 minutes

you will need for 4 servings:

4 oz. macaroni	salt, pepper
1 small onion, peeled and chopped	pinch basil
1 can condensed cream of tomato soup	1 tablespoon bread-crumbs
milk	2 tomatoes, peeled and sliced
4 oz. grated cheese	parsley

1 Cook macaroni with the onion in boiling salted water and drain well.

2 Heat the soup with ⅓ can milk, stir till almost boiling, then add macaroni and cheese, reserving 1 table-spoonful.

3 Add seasoning and basil and pour into a buttered fireproof dish.

4 Mix remaining cheese and breadcrumbs and sprinkle on top.

5 Arrange tomato slices round the edge and brown under the grill or in a hot oven.

6 Serve at once, garnished with parsley.

Pancakes

Cheese pancakes

cooking time: about 2 minutes for each pancake

you will need for 4 servings:

4 oz. flour	½ pint milk
¼ teaspoon salt	4 oz. grated cheese
1 egg, separated	butter for frying

Sieve flour and salt and make a well in the centre.

Add egg yolk and enough milk to make a smooth creamy batter.

Beat well, then add remaining milk and 2 oz. cheese.

Beat egg white stiffly and fold into batter.

Heat butter in a small frying pan and fry the pancakes in the usual way.

Sprinkle each with a little of the remaining cheese before rolling up.

Cheese and tomato pancakes

cooking time: 15–20 minutes

you will need for 4 servings:

for the batter:	
4 oz. flour	8 oz. grated cheese
pinch salt	8 oz. tomatoes, peeled and sliced thinly
1 egg	salt, pepper
½ pint milk	

1 Make batter (see page 90) and leave to stand for at least 1 hour, if possible in a cool place.

2 Make thin pancakes and pile on a hot dish, sprinkling each one with cheese and adding a few slices of tomato.

3 Season each layer carefully with a little salt and pepper.

4 Sprinkle remaining cheese on top of the last pancake. To serve, cut into wedges.

Macaroni and cheese pancake

cooking time: 25–30 minutes

you will need for 4 servings:

6 oz. macaroni	salt, pepper
2 oz. butter	2 eggs
3 oz. Gruyère cheese, grated	tomato sauce (see page 91)
2 oz. ham, minced or finely chopped	

1 Cook macaroni in boiling salted water for 15 minutes. Drain, chop and add 1 oz. butter.

2 Add cheese, ham, seasoning and beaten eggs.

3 Heat remaining butter in a pan, add macaroni mixture and cook till brown on one side.

4 Turn over* to brown other side. Serve with tomato sauce.

*If the pancake is difficult to turn, turn out on to a plate. Heat a little more butter in the pan, then replace the pancake to brown the underside.

Celery layer pancakes

cooking time: 15–20 minutes

you will need for 4 servings:

browned breadcrumbs	**for the sauce:**
4 eggs	1 oz. butter or margarine
1½ tablespoons flour	1 oz. flour
2 tablespoons milk	¼ pint celery liquid
salt	¼ pint milk
	salt, pepper
for the filling:	
1 small can celery hearts	2 oz. grated cheese
little margarine	

1 Grease 3 sandwich tins and sprinkle with breadcrumbs.

2 Separate the eggs. *continued*

3 Mix the flour, milk, salt and egg yolks together and beat well.

4 Whisk the egg whites until stiff and gently fold into the mixture.

5 Divide the mixture between the three tins and bake in a very moderate oven (325°F. – Gas Mark 3) until set.

6 Meanwhile, drain and chop the celery and heat it in the margarine.

7 Make the sauce by melting the margarine and adding the flour. Cook for 1–2 minutes and gradually add the celery liquid (from the tin) and the milk, stirring all the time.

8 Bring to the boil and season well.

9 Place one pancake on a hot dish and cover with hot celery.

10 Place a second pancake over it and sprinkle with grated cheese.

11 Top with third pancake and pour the sauce over the whole and sprinkle with grated cheese. Serve at once.

Pancakes au gratin

cooking time: about 15 minutes

you will need for 4 servings:

2 hard-boiled eggs	½ pint pancake batter
4 oz. cooked ham, chopped finely	(see page 90)
salt, pepper	1 tablespoon grated cheese
½ pint cheese sauce (see page 91)	

1 Chop eggs, mix with ham and season carefully. Bind with 1 tablespoon sauce.

2 Make the pancakes in the usual way, put a little of the filling on each and fold up.

3 When all the pancakes are cooked, arrange them in a fireproof dish. Coat with remaining sauce and sprinkle with cheese.

4 Heat through in a moderate oven (350°F. – Gas Mark 4).

Onion filled pancakes

cooking time: about 35 minutes

you will need for 4 servings:

1 large grated onion	2 chopped hard-boiled eggs
½ pint pancake batter (see page 90)	salt, pepper
8 oz. minced cooked vegetables	½ pint cheese sauce (see page 91)
	2 oz. grated cheese

1 Stir the onion into the pancake batter.

2 Fry the pancakes and keep them warm.

3 Mix the vegetables and eggs together adding salt and pepper.

4 Put an equal quantity on to each pancake and roll it up.

5 Arrange the pancakes in an ovenproof dish, pour on the cheese sauce and sprinkle with grated cheese.

6 Bake in a moderately hot oven (375°F. – Gas Mark 5) for 15 minutes.

Savoury pancake

cooking time: about 45 minutes

you will need for 4 servings:

8 oz. potatoes	salt, pepper
6 rashers streaky bacon	2 large or 3 small eggs
1 small onion, peeled and finely chopped	4–5 tablespoons milk
1 oz. grated cheese	1 oz. butter
1 tablespoon flour	3–4 tomatoes, grilled or baked

1 Peel and grate potatoes coarsely.

2 Remove rind from bacon, chop and add to potato with onion, cheese, flour and seasoning.

3 Mix all well together.

4 Beat eggs, add milk and stir into mixture.

5 Melt butter in a fireproof dish. Pour in mixture and bake about 45 minutes in a moderately hot oven (375°F. – Gas Mark 5).
Serve hot with tomatoes.

Potato pancakes

cooking time: 20 minutes

you will need for 4 servings:

1 lb. potatoes	butter or corn oil
1 medium onion	cheese sauce
2 eggs	tomato or spinach for serving
4 tablespoons flour	
salt, pepper	

1 Peel potatoes and grate coarsely. Drain off excess water.

2 Grate onion finely.

3 Mix potatoes and onion with eggs, lightly beaten.

4 Stir in flour with a good pinch of salt and pepper.

5 Drop heaped tablespoons of the mixture into hot butter or oil. Fry on both sides until brown, flattening pancakes with a knife as they cook.

6 Serve with cheese sauce and grilled tomatoes or spinach.

Florentine pancakes

cooking time: about 10 minutes for filling

you will need for 4 servings:

2 lb. spinach	½ pint pancake batter
salt, pepper	(see page 90)
nutmeg	8 oz. grated cheese
½ oz. butter	

1 Cook the spinach in the usual way, drain and chop very finely.

2 Add salt, pepper, nutmeg and butter.

3 Make the pancakes and pile on a hot dish, putting a layer of spinach and a very generous sprinkling of cheese on each pancake before stacking them.

4 Continue until the ingredients are used up, then top with grated cheese and serve cut into wedges.

Sandwiches

Sandwich fillings

Egg fillings

a Chop **hard-boiled eggs,** mix with chopped diced crisp **bacon** and a little salad dressing or mayonnaise.

b Chop **hard-boiled eggs,** mix with sweet **chutney** and chopped **watercress.**

c Scramble eggs, mix with chopped **chives** and a little sliced **tomato.**

d Chop **soft-boiled eggs** finely – mix with **butter** and seasoning.

e **Anchovy and egg,** blend 1 can anchovies, finely chopped, 4 chopped hard-boiled eggs, 1 tablespoon mayonnaise and 4 oz. luxury margarine.

Cheese fillings

a **Cream cheese,** mix with a little well-drained and finely chopped **pineapple.**

b **Cream cheese,** mix with chopped **walnuts,** spread on crisp lettuce.

c Slice of **Gruyère or Cheddar cheese** spread lightly with made **mustard** and sprigs of **watercress.**

d Grate **cheese,** mix with grated raw **carrot** and little **mayonnaise.**

e **Cheese and celery,** blend 4 oz. finely grated cheese, 2 finely chopped sticks of celery or 1 head of chicory, finely chopped, 4 oz. luxury margarine, seasoning.

Cheese sandwich filling

you will need for 4 sandwiches:

2 oz. butter	1 teaspoon horseradish
½ teaspoon salt	sauce or chutney
½ teaspoon made mustard	8 oz. grated cheese
few drops Worcestershire sauce	3–4 tablespoons milk

1 Beat butter till soft, add salt, mustard, sauce, horseradish or chutney and mix well.

2 Add cheese and enough milk to make a fairly soft smooth spread.

Chicken and cheese sandwich

you will need for 1 sandwich:

thin slices cold cooked chicken and ham	2 oz. cream cheese
3 rounds buttered bread	few capers, chopped

1 Arrange chicken and ham on one round of bread and cover with the second slice of bread.

2 Mix cheese with capers and spread on top.

3 Cover with third round of bread.

Club sandwich

you will need for 1 sandwich:

3 rounds bread	1–2 rashers bacon,
Cheddar cheese, cut into thin slices	grilled
mustard	lettuce
1 tomato, peeled and sliced thinly	salad cream

1 Toast the bread on both sides.

2 Cover one round with cheese and spread lightly with mustard. Arrange tomato slices on top.

3 Cover with the second round of toast. Put bacon on top and cover with lettuce and a little salad cream. Top with remaining toast.

Devilled cheese and ham sandwich

you will need for 4 servings:

8 oz. grated Cheddar cheese	2–3 tablespoons sour cream or salad cream
½ teaspoon dry mustard	(see page 89)
1 teaspoon Worcestershire sauce	butter
2 teaspoons horseradish cream	8 rounds bread
	4 slices cooked ham

1 Mix cheese, mustard, sauce and horseradish to a paste with sour cream or salad cream.

2 Spread on to 4 rounds buttered bread, place a slice of ham on top and complete the sandwiches with remaining buttered bread.

Ham and egg club sandwich, no. 1

you will need for 1 sandwich:

cooked ham	little grated cheese
little made mustard	scrambled egg (see page
3 rounds buttered bread	5)

1 Chop ham, mustard and spread on one round of bread. Cover with the second round.

2 Add some cheese to the well seasoned scrambled egg and spread on top.

3 Cover with the third round of bread.

Ham and egg club sandwich, no. 2

you will need for 1 sandwich:

1 slice ham
3 rounds buttered bread
made mustard
1 hard-boiled egg
mayonnaise or salad
    cream (see page 89)
salt, pepper

1 Put ham on one round of bread and spread lightly with mustard. Cover with second round of bread.
2 Chop the egg, bind with a little mayonnaise or salad cream and season to taste.
3 Spread on the second round of bread and cover with the third.

Guernsey sandwiches

cooking time: 6 minutes

you will need for 4 servings:

4 oz. Cheddar cheese
8 thin slices, cut from a
    small loaf
4 slices cooked ham
8 oz. tomatoes
pinch sugar
salt, pepper
1 level teaspoon made
    mustard
2 oz. butter
watercress, optional

1 Cut the cheese into thin slices. Use half to cover 4 slices of bread.

2 Lay a slice of ham over each, cover with sliced tomato. Sprinkle lightly with sugar, salt and pepper.
3 Top with remaining slices of cheese.
4 Thinly spread remaining slices of bread with mustard. Use to sandwich cheese layer.
5 Press sandwiches firmly together.
6 Fry in melted butter, for 3 minutes each side. Cut in half crosswise, serve at once, garnished with watercress, if liked.

Variation

Guernsey sandwiches with eggs – prepare as before, but do not cut through. Keep sandwiches hot. Fry 4 eggs in pan, adding more butter if required. Top each sandwich with a fried egg. Serves 4.

Cheese dishes for children

When a baby has been weaned, cheese should form part of its diet. It is especially good for children because it is rich in protein and calcium.
For very tiny children it is best to grate the cheese.

Cheese aigrettes

cooking time: 7–8 minutes

you will need for 4 servings:

¼ pint water
½ oz. butter
2 oz. flour
1 egg and 1 egg yolk
2 oz. grated Parmesan
    cheese
¼ teaspoon salt
pinch Cayenne pepper
fat for frying

1 Heat water and butter together slowly until the water boils and butter has melted.
2 Remove from heat, add flour and beat till smooth.
3 Return to heat and cook till mixture leaves the sides of the pan clean.
4 Cool a little, add eggs, most of the cheese and seasoning. Beat well.
5 Cook in teaspoonfuls in hot fat until well risen and golden brown. Do not cook too many at one time.
6 Drain well on absorbent paper and sprinkle with remaining cheese before serving.

Bread and cheese puff

cooking time: about 45 minutes

you will need for 4 servings:

8 ½-inch thick rounds
    stale bread
6 oz. cheese, sliced
3 eggs
½ pint milk
salt, Cayenne pepper
½ teaspoon paprika

1 Put bread and cheese in alternate layers in a buttered fireproof dish.
2 Beat eggs, add milk, seasoning and paprika and pour over bread and cheese.
3 Cover and chill thoroughly in the refrigerator.*
4 Stand the dish in a pan of hot water and cook in a moderate oven (350°F. – Gas Mark 4) for 45 minutes.

*This is important or the savoury will not puff up as it should.

Cheese fluff

cooking time: about 7 minutes

you will need for 1 serving:

2 oz. grated Cheddar
    cheese
2 tablespoons milk
1 egg, separated
2 rounds buttered toast

1 Put cheese with milk and stir over gentle heat until cheese has melted.

2 Add yolk and continue to cook very gently until mixture thickens.

3 Beat egg white stiffly and fold into mixture.

4 Put the toast into a buttered fireproof dish. Pour cheese mixture on top and brown lightly under the grill.

Cheese croquettes

cooking time: 5–6 minutes

you will need for 4 servings:

2 packets Demi-sel cheese	1 teaspoon chopped parsley
2 oz. grated Parmesan cheese	1 egg
1 tablespoon flour	egg and breadcrumbs for coating
Cayenne pepper	butter and oil for frying
pinch nutmeg	

1 Mix cheeses, flour, pepper, nutmeg and parsley.

2 Add beaten egg and mix all to a smooth paste.

3 With floured hands form into 8 small croquettes and coat with egg and breadcrumbs.

4 Heat about 2 oz. butter and 1 tablespoon oil and fry croquettes till brown on both sides.

5 Drain and serve hot with fried chicken or veal or cold with salad.

Cheese mousse

cooking time: about 10 minutes

you will need for 2 servings:

2 eggs	¼ pint thin cream
½ pint milk	¼ oz. gelatine
3 oz. grated cheese (Cheddar or Cheshire)	sliced tomato
salt, pinch Cayenne pepper	watercress

1 Separate eggs, mix yolks with milk and heat carefully, stirring all the time till custard thickens.

2 Stir in cheese and season lightly.

3 Cool a little, then add cream and the gelatine dissolved in 1 tablespoon hot water.

4 Lastly fold in stiffly beaten egg whites.

5 Pour into small dariole tins rinsed out with cold water and leave to set.

6 Serve garnished with tomato slices and watercress.

Cheese niblets

cooking time: 3–4 minutes

you will need for 2 servings:

1 egg	fingers of bread about ½-inch thick
2 tablespoons Cheddar cheese, finely grated	butter
5–6 tablespoons milk	

1 Beat egg, add cheese and milk.

2 Put fingers of bread into a shallow dish, pour egg and cheese mixture over and leave until bread is thoroughly soaked.

3 Heat butter until it just begins to colour, then fry the fingers of bread on both sides until lightly browned.

Cheese pudding

cooking time: about 35 minutes

you will need for 4 servings:

1 pint milk	1 teaspoon made mustard
3 oz. freshly made breadcrumbs	1 teaspoon chopped chives
2 eggs, separated	4 oz. grated cheese
salt, freshly ground black pepper	

1 Heat milk to just below boiling point and pour over breadcrumbs. Soak about 20 minutes.

2 Add egg yolks, seasoning, chives and most of the cheese. Beat well.

3 Beat egg whites stiffly and fold into mixture.

4 Turn into a buttered fireproof dish, sprinkle remaining cheese on top and bake in a moderately hot oven (400°F. – Gas Mark 6) till brown and well risen (about 30 minutes).

Cheese savoury

cooking time: 20–25 minutes

you will need for 2 servings:

2 eggs	salt, pepper
4 oz. grated Lancashire cheese	pinch Cayenne pepper
¼ pint thick cream	pinch grated nutmeg

1 Beat eggs.

2 Add most of the cheese, cream and seasoning.

3 Add nutmeg.

4 Mix well and pour into a small casserole.

5 Sprinkle with remaining cheese and bake about 20–25 minutes in a moderately hot oven (400°F. – Gas Mark 6).

Serve hot with toast or a green salad.

Cheese soup

cooking time: about 6 minutes

you will need for 4 servings:

1 small onion, peeled and sliced very thinly	¼ pint white stock or water
1 oz. butter	salt, pepper
¾ oz. cornflour	4 oz. Cheddar cheese, diced
½ pint milk	

1 Cook onion in butter until transparent.

2 Add cornflour, mix well and cook for 1 minute.

3 Add milk, stock and seasoning, stir till boiling and boil for 5 minutes.

4 Add cheese, stir till melted, then serve at once.

Cheese triangles

cooking time: about 9 minutes

you will need for 4 servings:

1 pint milk	1 tablespoon chopped
1 small onion, peeled and	parsley
stuck with 1 clove	salt, Cayenne pepper
1 bay leaf	1 egg
6 peppercorns	1 dessertspoon oil
4 oz. semolina	breadcrumbs
4 oz. grated cheese	fat for deep frying

1 Put the milk with onion, bay leaf and peppercorns in a saucepan. Bring very slowly to boiling point, cover and leave for 15 minutes.
2 Strain milk, return to the pan and sprinkle semolina in. Stir till boiling, then simmer until semolina is cooked (about 6 minutes).
3 Remove from heat, add cheese, parsley and seasoning and beat well.
4 Turn out on to a wetted plate. Smooth the top with a wet knife and work into 8 triangles. Leave to get cold.
5 Beat egg with oil, brush each triangle with egg mixture and coat with breadcrumbs.
6 Fry in deep fat till crisp and golden brown. Serve with tomato sauce and a green vegetable, or with salad.

Egg and cheese fricassée (1)

cooking time: 10–15 minutes

you will need for 4 servings:

4 hard-boiled eggs	breadcrumbs
½ pint white sauce (see	½ oz. butter
page 91)	1–2 tomatoes, peeled
salt, pepper	and sliced
nutmeg	
4 tablespoons grated	
cheese	

1 Slice eggs and put into a buttered fireproof dish.
2 Make sauce, season carefully, add pinch nutmeg and 3 tablespoons grated cheese. Pour over the eggs.
3 Mix a few breadcrumbs with remaining cheese and sprinkle on top of the sauce.
4 Dot with butter and arrange slices of tomato round the edge of the dish.
5 Put into a moderately hot oven (400°F. – Gas Mark 6) for about 10 minutes.

Individual cheese eggs

cooking time: 4–5 minutes

you will need for 1 serving:

butter	salt, pepper
1 egg	½–¾ oz. grated cheese

1 Butter a small cocotte or ramekin dish and break the egg into it.
2 Season lightly and cover with cheese, dot with butter.
3 Grill until egg is lightly cooked.

Savoury egg filling for vol-au-vent cases

cooking time: approx. 10 minutes

you will need:

5 eggs	seasoning
3 tablespoons cream or	2 oz. diced lean tongue
mayonnaise	or ham
1 oz. butter	

1 Beat the eggs and cream or mayonnaise together.
2 Heat the butter, add the eggs and season to taste. Cook over a gentle heat, stirring, until the mixture thickens.
3 When the mixture has thickened to a creamy consistency, remove from heat, but allow to continue to thicken in heat of the pan.
4 Stir in the chopped tongue or ham.
5 Spoon in hot vol-au-vent cases and serve at once.

Savoury rice

cooking time: 35–40 minutes

you will need for 4 servings:

2 oz. butter	1 teaspoon horseradish
1 large onion, peeled and	cream
chopped	½ pint cheese sauce (see
4 oz. rice	page 91)
1 chicken stock cube	4 tomatoes, halved and
¾ pint boiling water	grilled
6 hard-boiled eggs	3–4 stuffed olives

1 Melt butter, add onion and cook till transparent.
2 Add rice and continue cooking till onion begins to brown and rice grains are opaque.
3 Dissolve stock cube in boiling water and stir into rice mixture. Simmer till rice is tender and stock absorbed.
4 Arrange rice in a ring in a serving dish.
5 Cut eggs into quarters and pile in the centre.
6 Add horseradish to sauce and pour over eggs.
7 Arrange tomatoes round the edge and garnish rice with sliced olives.

Bean and sausage crumble

cooking time: 30 minutes

you will need for 4 servings:

1 10½-oz. can cream of	**crumble topping:**
tomato soup	3 oz. flour
1 16-oz. can baked beans	salt, pepper
with sausages	2 oz. margarine
	2 oz. grated cheese

1 Mix the soup with the beans and sausages and put in an ovenproof dish.
2 Sieve the flour and seasoning into a bowl.
3 Rub in the margarine, add the cheese and mix well.
4 Sprinkle the mixture over the beans and sausages and bake moderately hot (400°F. – Gas Mark 6).

Drinks for invalids

It is important that an invalid should have plenty of liquid in the form of various kinds of drinks. The following recipes made with eggs will provide nourishment and tempt an invalid's poor appetite.

Egg cognac

no cooking

you will need for 1 serving:
3 egg yolks	1 wine glass cognac
1 tablespoon sugar	

Beat yolks and sugar. Add cognac. Chill before serving.

Egg flip

cooking time: few minutes

you will need for 1 serving:
1 egg	½ pint milk
1 teaspoon sugar	flavouring to taste

1 Separate egg and mix sugar with yolk.
2 Heat milk and pour on to the yolk.
3 Strain yolk mixture and stir in the egg white, beaten until just frothy.
4 Flavour with nutmeg, vanilla essence or sherry.

Egg grog

no cooking

you will need for 1 serving:
1 egg	hot water
2 teaspoons sugar	1 slice lemon
1 wine glass rum	

1 Lightly beat the egg.
2 Beat in the sugar, add rum.
3 Add hot water as required and serve with a lemon slice.

Egg lemonade

no cooking

you will need for 1 serving:
1 egg	pinch nutmeg
1 tablespoon sugar	water or soda water
juice of 1 lemon	

1 Beat egg with sugar.
2 Add lemon juice and nutmeg.
3 Add water or soda water as required.

Egg nog

cooking time: few minutes

you will need for 1 serving:
2 eggs	½ pint milk
1 teaspoon sugar	flavouring to taste

1 Beat eggs and sugar with a little milk until well blended.
2 Warm remaining milk to blood heat and pour over egg mixture.
3 Strain, then flavour to taste with sherry, brandy, rum, vanilla essence or nutmeg.

Egg punch

cooking time: few minutes

you will need for 1 serving:
1 egg	1 wine glass brandy or
1 teaspoon sugar	rum
	¼ pint milk

1 Beat egg with sugar.
2 Add brandy or rum.
3 Heat milk to just below boiling point and pour over the egg.
4 Stir well and serve hot.

All about cheese

How English cheese is made

There are many varieties of cheese manufactured in Britain today. In the past goats' milk was used but today cows' milk is used in the manufacture of cheese. The flavour and texture of the cheese are largely governed by the method of manufacture and to some extent, by the area in which cows graze.

The first cheese factory was established in England about one hundred years ago. During the middle 1930s there were about a thousand cheese-making farms in the United Kingdom but there has been a sharp decrease in the number of farms making cheese during the past 30 years. At the present time there are a little over 200 cheese-making farms.

The first stage of cheese-making is the process of clotting the milk. This process is speeded up by adding a liquid known as a *starter* (a culture containing bacteria). In an hour or so, the milk is sour enough for 'renneting'. Rennet must also be added to the milk containing starter; when rennet is added the milk is turned into a clotted part, the *curd*, and a watery part, the *whey*. Cheese is made from the curd. After about 45 minutes, the curd is like solid junket, and is cut, by means of special knives, into small pieces, then heat is applied so that even more of the watery whey content is removed. In the end there remains a springy, spongy, but more or less solid block of curd. This is cut into blocks and drained and pressed to remove almost all the remainder of the whey and again cut up into blocks. These are piled on top of each other and turned at regular intervals. During this time the acidity in the curd is being checked and tested. In the end the curd should be about 5 times as acidic as the original milk. Next the curd is cut up by means of a mechanical grinder and salted – the salt is added to give flavour to the cheese and it also acts as a preservative. The curd is then packed into cloth-lined moulds, each containing about 65–80 lb. of cheese. The last of the whey is then pressed out, and hot water is sprayed on the moulds, thus producing a thin, hard rind on the cheese, which helps to keep it. After this the cheeses, as they have now become, are put into powerful presses, and left for 24 hours under a pressure of 10–12 tons. Finally the cheeses are stamped with the date, and taken to the ripening room and left to mature for about four months. During this time they are turned daily in an atmosphere where the temperature and dampness are carefully controlled.

The following table gives brief notes on colour, texture and flavour of British cheeses, which will be a helpful guide when buying cheese.

VARIETY	APPEARANCE		FLAVOUR	AGE WHEN READY FOR EATING
	Colour	Texture		
Caerphilly	White	Close	Mild	2 weeks
Cheddar	White	Close	Mellow	3 months
Cheshire	Red and white	Loose and crumbly	Mild and mellow	6 weeks
	Blue	Close	Rich and creamy	6 months
Derby	White	Buttery and open	Tangy	4–6 weeks
Dorset Blue Vinny	Blue	Crumbly	Strong and rich	4–6 months
Double Gloucester	Pale straw colour	Buttery and open	Mellow and full	3–4 months
Lancashire	White	Buttery and open. Crumbly	Mild	4–8 weeks
Leicester	Red	Buttery and open	Medium strong	10–12 weeks
Stilton	White	Open	Mild	3 weeks
	Blue	Open	Rich and mellow	3–6 months
Wensleydale	White	Moderately close	Mild and slightly salty	3 weeks
	Blue	Soft and close	Rich, sweet and creamy	6 months

ABC of cheeses

As there are some 400 different cheeses made in France alone, it would be quite impossible to list them all. However, I have included the most appreciated French cheeses (some of which are available in this country) as well as the English ones and some of those from other lands.

Autun – this is known as 'cow cheese' and can be eaten all the year round.

(Les) Aydes – a cheese from the Orléannais district of France. It is best eaten from October to June.

Banon – a cheese made in Provence, in the foothills of the Alps. It is best eaten from May to November.

Bleu d'Auvergne – a blue mould cheese made usually from a mixture of goats', ewes' and cows' milk. It is also known as *Bleu de Salers*. It is best eaten from November to May.

Bleu de Basillac – a cheese similar to *Roquefort* made in Limousin. It is best eaten from November to May.

Blue mould French cheeses
(Bleus Français) – there are a number of these cheeses in France which are similar to *Roquefort*, but which have a less delicate flavour. Among the best of these are: *Bleu d'Auvergne, Fourme d'Ambert, Champoleon, Saint-Marcellin, Sassenage,* and *Sept-moncel.*

Blue cheeses from other lands
A great number of blue mould cheeses come from countries other than France. They include *Tyrolean blue* from Rastadt, *Cabrales* from the Asturias, *Castello-branco* from Portugal, *Sarrazin* from Sarraz in Switzerland, *Stilton* from England and *Stracchino* from Italy. The latter is similar to *Gorgonzola.*

Bondon – a cheese which is made in Normandy, mostly around Rouen. It is a small loaf-shaped cheese about 3-inches high and from 1 to 2-inches in diameter.

Bosson Macéré – a French cheese made in Provence. It is best eaten from December to March.

(La) Bouille – a cheese made in Normandy. It is best eaten from October to May.

Boule de Lille – a Dutch cheese known in Holland as *Oude Kass.* This cheese can be eaten all the year round.

Brie – this cheese has a claim to nobility so I think a little more must be said about it. In the fifteenth century, Charles d'Orléans, who was the father of Louis XII, used to order Bries by the dozen to give as New Year presents to his friends.
Brie is made in various sizes – a large Brie may be up to 22-inches in diameter, a medium Brie up to 16-inches and a small one about 13-inches.
Brie is fully ripe when the cheese is all of the same texture. When pressure is exerted on the surface of a section the cheese should bulge, but not run out.
A good Brie must have a reddish crust with a few traces of white, but no blackish streaks. It must be creamy but not runny, and should be pale yellow in colour.
There are different kinds of Brie, some of which are described.

Brie de Coulommiers – the difference between this and and the usual Brie is that a little cream is often added to it, to soften it. If the cheese is to be eaten fresh, more cream is added to it than if it is to be left to mature.

Brie de Melun – also known as *Brie d'amateur.* It is made in smaller and thicker rounds than the usual Brie. It has a more pronounced aroma, being saltier and more piquant.

Brie de Provins – a little different in shape from the usual Brie, being thicker and small in circumference. Brie is a cheese which is best eaten from November to May.

Brizen – this is a cheese from Hungary, made from ewes' milk.

Broccio – a cheese made in Corsica from goats' milk and sour ewes' milk. It has a very delicate flavour and similar in appearance to '*Petit-Suisse*'. A large proportion of this cheese is exported. It is eaten plain or in fritters or ravioli. It is also used as a stuffing for vegetables. A special cake called *Fiadene* is also made from it.

Caccio-Cavallo – a cheese made in Italy in the region

of Naples, from skimmed cows' milk. It is moulded into the shape of gourds and left to dry on sticks. Some Caccio-Cavallo addicts are not satisfied with having this cheese just dried but insist on it being smoke-cured as well, as was done far back in the time of the Romans.

Cachat – a cheese which is very popular in Provence, made from ewes' milk, ripened with vinegar, then pressed. It is best eaten from May to November.

Caerphilly – this cheese originated in a little Glamorgan village that gave it its name. Originally a miners' cheese, taken down to the coal face every day by pitmen. Its popularity spread and now it is manufactured mainly in Somerset, Wiltshire, Devon and Dorset. Caerphilly ripens quickly and should be eaten soon after buying.

Camembert – a cheese similar to *Brie* and should, I think, have a little more space devoted to it. A soft cheese made from whole unskimmed milk. It was invented in about 1790 by a local farmer's wife, Mme Harel. A statue has been erected to her in the little village of Camembert.
Camembert is a disc-shaped cheese, thicker and much smaller than Brie made in the Vimoutiers and Livarot regions of France. Like Brie, its crust must be reddish without any traces of black. The cheese must be pale yellow, smooth and without any holes. It must not be runny.
Although Camembert is made today all over France and even in other countries it is stipulated by law that its place of origin must be indicated.
Camembert is best eaten from October to June.

Cancoillotte – a very strong cheese made in Franche-Comté. Before being served this cheese has to be melted. It is best eaten from September to June.

Cantal – this is a hard, strong cheese made in the Auvergne district of France. It is also known as *Fourme de Sales*. It can be eaten the whole year round, but is at its best when eaten between November and May.

Chabichou – a soft, sweet goats' milk cheese which is best eaten from April to December.

Chabissous or Cabelous – these are little cheeses made from goats' or ewes' milk.

Cheddar – Cheddar cheese has been made in the shadow of the Mendip Hills, close by the towering Cheddar Gorge, since the sixteenth century. It is the 'prodigious cheese of delicate taste' of which William Camden wrote in the days of the first Elizabeth. Nowadays it is made, too, in Wiltshire, Dorset and elsewhere.

Chevret – a cheese from goats' milk which is best eaten from December to April.

Chevrotins – the name given to a cheese produced in Savoy. It is made from dried goats' milk and is best eaten from March to December.

Chevrotton de Mâcon – a cheese which is also known as *Mâconnais* which is best eaten from May to September.

Cierp de Luchon – a cheese made in the Comté de Foix which is best eaten from November to May.

Comté – a cheese made in Jura which can be eaten all the year round.

Coulommiers – comes into the category of soft cheeses, made in the district of Brie in the neighbourhood of Coulommiers. These cheeses are usually eaten after salting, but they may be also kept until they are covered with a white mould.
A good Coulommiers must have a white crust with a slight greyish tinge. It must be creamy to the touch and be slightly yellow in colour inside.

Cream cheese (Fromage à la Crème) – cream cheese can be made either by adding double cream to the milk, before introducing the rennet or it may be made from milk which has been completely skimmed; fresh cream is then worked in after draining, and the cheese moulded to complete the drainage.

Crème de Vosages – Alsatian soft cream cheese which is best eaten from October to April.

Crottin de Chavignol – a semi-hard cheese made in Berry from goats' milk. It is best eaten from May to December.

Dauphin – a cheese made in the North of France which is best eaten from November to May.

Decize – a cheese resembling *Brie*, which can be eaten all the year round.

Demi-Sel – this is a small whole-milk soft cheese similar to double cream. After the curd has been drained and sieved it is put into moulds and has 1–1·5% salt added to it.

Dorset blue vinny – this is a very rare cheese virtually unknown outside the county. Virile and pungent, it is the trickiest of English cheese to make.

Double-cream (Double-crème) – this is French soft cream cheese. The milk used is enriched with added cream. A small quantity of rennet is mixed with it so that the coagulation process lasts about 24 hours. The curd is wrapped in a cloth and put under weights to drain. More cream is worked in at this stage. The curds are then moulded and wrapped in waxed paper.

Double Gloucester – this cheese comes from Gloucester and was once garlanded and carried round the town in May Day processions. Charles Lamb considered it without rival as a supper cheese. The small single Gloucester is still seen, though rare.

Dunlop – this is a cheese made in Scotland and is similar to *Cheshire* and *Double Gloucester*, although in the opinion of English gastronomes it is far superior to both.

Dutch cheeses – there are a great many Dutch cheeses, the best known being *Edam* made also in a number of European countries as well as America. When fully fermented, the cheese made from partly skimmed milk, is painted over with a coating of linseed oil. Sometimes it is given a further coating of paraffin. The cheese is coloured with a dye, annatto.

Emmenthal – a hard cheese made all over Switzerland where there is high pasture land and named after the high Emme Valley. It is made from whole milk and manufactured in the same way as *Gruyère* although it is less pungent and usually less salty than *Gruyère*. It has holes in it known as 'eyes'. These are fairly large, but should not exceed a sixpence in diameter.

Epoisses – a whole milk soft cheese made in almost every part of Burgundy and in central France. Its name comes from a village on the Côte d'Or.
A special rennet flavoured with black pepper, clove, fennel, salt and brandy is added to the milk to curdle it. This cheese is eaten either fresh or ripened. It is left in cellars to ripen according to how it is to be eaten. If it is to be eaten over-ripe it is left for a longer time than if it is to be eaten runny.
The fresh cheese is eaten in the summer and the ripe in the winter or spring – November to June.

Etuvé – a semi-hard Dutch cheese which is good eaten all the year round.

Foutina – a soft, creamy cheese from Italy. It is used for making a kind of fondue in the Val d'Aosta.

Friesche Kaas – a soft Dutch cheese which is best eaten from November to May.

Frinot – a cheese made in the Orléans region which is best eaten from November to June.

Fromage à la Pie (Fresh unfermented cheese) – this is a cheese made usually on farms from skimmed milk and needs to be eaten immediately. It can be made in the home from whole milk, by leaving the milk to stand in a warm place (60–70°F.). After 24–36 hours the milk is curdled by the addition of rennet. This cheese is eaten when fresh with fresh cream added. If liked it may be seasoned with sugar or salt and pepper, according to taste, and a few chopped chives for added flavour.

Géromé – a cheese made from whole milk in Vosges. It is ripened in cellars for 4 months – after which time the crust is tawny in colour. Aniseed, fennel or caraway seeds are sometimes added. This cheese is best eaten from November to April.

Gervais – is a well-known make of *Petit-Suisse*.

Gex – this is a French blue-veined cheese made at Gex, the principal town of the Ain district. It is made from unskimmed whole milk. Before it is sold this cheese is ripened in cellars for two weeks. The 'blue' is due to the *Penicillum glaucum*, which is self-generating and appears during processing without aid from any foreign body.
The chief characteristic of this cheese, which distinguishes it from all others (apart from the blue streaks) is that it remains pure white.

Gjetöst – this is a brown-coloured cheese from Norway made from goats' milk.

Gorgonzola – this is a semi-hard Italian cheese which takes its name from a village near Milan. Good Gorgonzola should have a thin rind, be yellowish white in colour, and streaked, but not excessively with blue.

Gouda – a cheese similar to *Cantal* made in Holland from whole milk.

Gournay – a whole-milk soft cheese made at Gournay in Normandy and in the neighbouring districts.

Gruyère – this is a cheese manufactured in the mountains, close to the pastures of French Switzerland. This cheese is often confused with *Emmenthal*, but the 'eyes' in Gruyère are smaller than in *Emmenthal*. Gruyère will keep for a long time uncut. Some like this cheese fresh whereas others prefer it ripe. For fondue a mixture of the two kinds is normally required.

Gruyère (Crème de) – there has been on the market for several years now triangles of processed cheese wrapped in silver paper. At one time this cheese was produced mainly as a way of using up defective cheeses. Due to the fact that it has become so popular it is now manufactured from cheese made especially for the purpose.

Guerbigny – this is a cheese from Picardy which is best eaten from October to May.

Guéret – this cheese, sometimes known as *Creusois* is made in Guéret, a city in the Creuse district.

Hervé – this is a soft, fermented cheese made in Belgium from cows' milk. Hervé is made with either extra cream, cream or partly skimmed milk. It is turned out into cubes, ripened in cellars and wrapped in cloths which have been steeped in beer.

Huppemeau – a cheese similar to *Brie* made in the Loire-et-Cher region of France.

Jonchée – this is a cheese made from either ewes' or goats' milk. Half the milk is boiled with bay leaves. This is then mixed with the remainder of the raw milk. After being curdled with rennet it is decanted into little pots.

Kummel – a cheese made in Holland, with caraway seeds. It can be eaten all the year round and is also known under the name of *Leidsche Kaas*.

Leicester – this is like a large millstone in shape. It has a mild, mellow flavour and its russet colouring looks particularly well on the board.

Levroux – this is a cheese made in and around Berry from goats' milk. It is best eaten from May to December.

Leyden – this cheese is made in the same way as *Edam* and often flavoured with cumin, cloves or cinnamon. It is also known under the names of *Leidsche Kaas* and *Kummel*.

Limbourger – a semi-hard fermented cheese made in

Belgium as well as Alsace and Germany. It is made from whole-milk curds kneaded with chives, parsley and tarragon, after which it is put into moulds and dried in the sun. The surface of this cheese is made non-porous by salting and brushing.

Livarot – this soft paste cheese takes its name from a small town in the Calvados region of France. The cheese is usually coloured a brown or deep red. It is only good to eat between February and June, and is at its best February and March.

Malakoff – a cheese similar to *Neufchâtel*. It is made in disc shapes 2 inches in diameter and from $\frac{1}{3}$–$\frac{1}{2}$-inch thick.

Mariolles – this cheese takes its name from a village in the Avesnes district of France, but is in fact manufactured in Thiérache and all over Picardy. This cheese, also known as *Marolles* or *Marole*, is square in shape. The whole-milk curds are salted, dried very quickly and then stored in a cellar, where at frequent intervals they are washed with beer. It is best eaten from November to June.

Mont-Cenis – a cheese somewhere between a *Roquefort* and a *Gorgonzola*. It is a large, round, semi-hard, blue-veined cheese made from fresh whole milk. It is placed in cellars to ripen from where it acquires its characteristic blue streaks.

Mont d'Or – the cheese of this name manufactured today has very little resemblance to the original. It was at one time made along the banks of the Sâone round Lyons. It was made only from the milk of stable-fed goats and was ripened in cellars for 5 to 6 weeks.
Today it is made almost all over France and is manufactured from cows' milk. It is best eaten from December to April.

(La) Mothe-Sainte-Héraye – a cheese from Poitou made from goats' milk. It is also known as *Lamothe-Bougon*. It is best eaten from May to November.

Munster cheese – this is a semi-hard, fermented cheese made from whole milk in Alsace in the Munster Valley. It is much prized by cheese lovers. It is usually flavoured with caraway or anise seeds. It is best eaten from November to April.

Mysöst – this is a cheese from Norway and can be eaten all the year round.

Nantais – this cheese comes from Breton and is sometimes known as *fromage de curé*. It can be eaten all the year round.

Neufchâtel or Bondon – this is a small loaf-shaped cheese made from skimmed milk, whole milk or with added cream, according to the type of cheese required. It is ripened in a drying room on bundles of straw, until a skin forms on the surface (this is known as the first skin). The ripening process is then completed in cool, well-aired store-rooms until a second skin forms. The second skin is reddish in colour and the cheese a dark yellow colour.

Olivet – a cheese made in the small town of Olivet in the Loiret from ewes' milk. It is best eaten from October to June.

Oloron – a cheese from Béarn. It is also known as *fromage de la Vallée d'Ossau*. This cheese should be eaten from October to May.

Paladru – a cheese made in Savoy. It is best eaten from November to May.

Parmesan – this famous long-keeping cheese is made in Lombardy and in the Romagna under various names. The name 'Parmesan' is used abroad for export cheeses of this type. Parmesan is made with skimmed milk. It is a very hard cheese, golden yellow in colour and can be eaten all the year round.

Pelardon de Ruoms – a cheese made from goats' milk in Ardèche in France. It is best eaten from May to November.

Petit-Carré – this cheese has the same flavour and texture as *Malakoff*. It is square in shape, 2-inches across and approximately ½-inch thick.

Petit-Suisse – a small cylindrical-shaped cheese of the double cream variety. It is made from whole milk with 20% proportion of fresh cream added. It was first made in Gournay in Normandy not in Switzerland as its name suggests.

Pithiviers au Foin – a cheese made in the Orléans region of France. The cheese is ripened on hay. It is best eaten from October to May.

Pontgibaud cheese (Puy-de-Dôme) – this cheese is made the same way as *Roquefort*, but from cows' milk. This cheese can be eaten all the year round, except in mid-summer.

Pont l'Evêque – this is a semi-hard French cheese made from whole or skimmed milk. The cheese is shaped in square moulds, salted and processed like *Neufchâtel*. It is ripened from 3–4 months in cellars. The ripening time may be a little less if the cheese is very rich in cream. This cheese should be softish and pale yellow in colour; the crust should be wrinkled and greyish yellow. This cheese is good to eat all the year round, except during August.

Port-Salut – this is a cheese made from whole milk and is creamy yellow in colour.
This cheese was first made at the Trappist Monastery of Port du Salut near Laval. It got its name from a company established at Entrammes, where it is still made. It is made in Trappist Monasteries all over the world according to a secret formula.

Pultöst – a cheese made in the mountain-farms of Norway which can be eaten all the year round.

Reblochon – a soft cheese made in Savoy from ewes' milk. It is best eaten from October to June.

Remondou – a cheese made in Belgium. It is also known as *Fromage piquant*! It is best eaten from November to June.

Riceys Cendré – a cheese sometimes called *Champensis*, which is best eaten from September to June.

Rigotte de Condrieu – this is a semi-hard cheese made in the Lyons district from goats' milk. It is best eaten from May to November.

Rocamadour – a small cheese made from ewes' milk and weighs only about 2 oz.

Rollot – a disc-shaped cheese from Picardy similar to *Brie* and *Camembert*, although smaller. It is also known as *Bigolot*. It is best eaten from October to May.

Romalour – this is a cheese from the Loire district of France which can be eaten all the year round.

Roquefort – the true Roquefort cheese is made from ewes' milk in a little town of that name in the Saint-Affrique district. The reason for ewes' milk being used is that sheep are the only animals which can subsist on the arid pastures.
The unique feature of this cheese is that the curds are mixed with a special type of breadcrumb. To ensure the right ripening conditions the cheeses are stored in damp, cool caves (40–48°F.), such as the natural

caves found in the Causses region.

In the view of the experts Roquefort should be kept for a year, but it is ready for the consumer after 30 to 40 days. A good Roquefort has a greyish rind, the cheese itself is yellow in colour and evenly veined with blue. The cheese has not been properly fermented if it is too white in appearance and chalky in texture.

The Roquefort 'season' lasts from May to September. A number of Roquefort-type cheeses are produced in different regions of France, but they may not be sold under the name of Roquefort.

Rougeret – a small cheese made from goats' milk near Mâcon. It is also known as *Maconnet*.

Sage Derby – this is a rare cheese, flavoured with chopped sage, and has long been a delicacy at Christmas time.

Saint-Agathon – a cheese from Breton which is best eaten from October to July.

Saint-Florentin – this is a soft, salty cheese from Burgundy. It is best eaten from November to July.

Saint-Marcellin – this is a cheese which was made exclusively from goats' milk and manufactured chiefly at Saint-Marcellin, the principal town of the Isère district. Today both cows' and ewes' milk are added or are used as a substitute for the goats' milk.

Saint-Maure – a soft creamy cheese made from goats' milk. It is best eaten from May to November.

Saint-Rémi – a square, soft cheese similar to *Pont-l'Evêque* made in Franche-Comté and Haute-Savoie.

Sassenage – this is a semi-hard, blue-veined cheese made in the Isère district. It is best eaten from November to May.

Septmoncel – this cheese is made in the same way as *Gex* cheese. The curds from two milkings are sometimes put together without mixing to produce a cheese known as *bastard Septmoncel*.

Soumaintrim – this cheese is also called *Saint-Florentin*. It is made in Burgundy and regarded as the prime vintage among all those made in the Armance valley in Burgundy.

This is a round yellow cheese, with a yellowish orange rind weighing approximately one pound. It is best eaten from November to July.

Soya – a cheese which has been made in China from time immemorial and is the result of fermentation in the juices extracted from soya beans.

After the soya beans have been softened and swollen by soaking, they are pressed through a sieve. The resulting liquid is mixed with a little sulphate of lime or magnesium. It coagulates into a grey mass, which is left to ferment like the curds in the cheese industry.

Stilton – Stilton known as King. Stilton is difficult to manufacture and therefore is only made by enthusiasts. It is made from whole milk with cream added. It comes from Melton Mowbray, from Hartington in the Dove Valley and from the Vale of Belvoir. It starts its life as White Stilton and matures into the famous Blue, first sold over 100 years ago to coach passengers at the Bell Inn at Stilton Village, which was on the Great North Road.

Stracchino – this is a soft Italian cheese made from goats' milk.

Strong cheese (Fromage Fort) – the cheese which is exceedingly savoury and strong smelling is particularly well liked in the Morvan and Lyons districts. Layer upon layer of grated or thinly sliced milk cheese, salt and mixed herbs, and sometimes a little cream are put into stoneware jars. The jars are then filled to the top with white wine and brandy. They are hermetically sealed and left to ferment in a warm place for two to three weeks.

Tête de Mort – this is the name given in France to the *Edam* cheese from Holland.

Tomme – this is a cheese of the Savoy. There are several varieties: *Tomme de Beauges* and *Tomme au fenouil* which are best eaten from September to June; *Tomme de Boudave* which is best eaten from October to July. *Tomme aux Raisins* is a small round cheese covered with grape pips.

Troyes – this is a soft, creamy cheese similar to Camembert. It is also known as *Barberey*. It is best eaten from November to May.

Vacherin – this is a soft cheese made in the Jura in Switzerland and in Franche-Comté. It is best eaten from November to May.

Valençay – this is a soft cheese, made from goats' milk, in the Berry district. It is best eaten from May to December.

Vendôme – this is a soft cheese made in Orléans. It is best eaten from October to June.

Wensleydale – this cheese has a delicious honeyed after-taste, redolent of the lush pastureland that produces it. It is thought that the Cistercian monks of Jervaulx Abbey brought their famous cheese to Wensleydale in early times. When Henry VIII pillaged their property the monks fled, leaving their precious recipe in the hands of the farmers' wives.

Recipes for reference

Anchovy butter

you will need:

5–6 anchovy fillets	lemon juice
2 oz. butter	cochineal (optional)

1 Wash anchovies to remove some of the salt, then pat dry.
2 Pound well with butter and a squeeze of lemon juice and then rub through a fine sieve.
3 Add a few drops cochineal.

Cooked salad cream

cooking time: 3 minutes

you will need:

1 tablespoon cornflour	paprika
2 teaspoons sugar	1 egg yolk
1 teaspoon dry mustard	6 tablespoons corn oil
salt	¼ pint sour cream
pepper	3 tablespoons vinegar

1 Mix cornflour, sugar, mustard and seasoning.
2 Stir in the egg yolk, corn oil and cream.
3 Mix well together, and boil gently for 3 minutes, stirring constantly.
4 Remove from heat, stir in the vinegar. Chill before using.

Cooked salad dressing

cooking time: few minutes

you will need:

½ pint fairly thick white sauce (see page 91)	2 tablespoons malt vinegar
2 egg yolks	1 tablespoon tarragon vinegar
salt, pepper	

1 Make sauce and remove from heat. Stir in beaten yolks and season to taste.
2 Cook very gently over a low heat. Do not boil.
3 Stir in vinegars and use as required.
This dressing will keep for a short time, stored in a cool place.

Cream salad dressing

you will need:

¼ teaspoon made mustard	1 tablespoon oil
¼ teaspoon salt	1 dessertspoon vinegar (a mixture of malt and tarragon)
pepper	
pinch castor sugar	
2 tablespoons thick cream	

1 Mix mustard, salt, pepper to taste and sugar.
2 Stir in the cream.
3 Add oil drop by drop, stirring all the time.
4 Add the vinegar slowly and stir well.

Salad cream

cooking time: few minutes

you will need:

½ pint fairly thick white sauce (see page 91)	2 tablespoons malt vinegar
2 egg yolks	1 tablespoon tarragon vinegar
salt, pepper	

1 Make the sauce and remove from heat. Stir in beaten egg yolks and season to taste.
2 Cook very gently over a low heat. Do not boil.
3 Stir in the vinegars and use as required.
This salad cream will keep for a short time, if it is stored in a cool place.

Never-fail mayonnaise

you will need:

¾ teaspoon sugar	1 egg white
¼ teaspoon dry mustard	6 tablespoons corn oil
salt, pepper	3 teaspoons vinegar

1 Mix sugar, mustard, salt and pepper. Blend in the egg white and beat well.
2 Continue beating, adding the corn oil a little at a time, until half is used.
3 Add 2 teaspoons vinegar, then remaining corn oil, beating all the time.
4 Beat in remaining vinegar.

Note: The mayonnaise may be stored in a covered jar in the refrigerator. These quantities make about ¼ pint.

French dressing

you will need:

1 tablespoon oil	¼ teaspoon salt
pinch pepper	1 tablespoon malt or
pinch dry mustard	wine vinegar

1 Mix oil and seasoning, add vinegar.

Note: Stir before using as the ingredients separate.

Pancake batter

you will need:

8 oz. plain flour	2 eggs
¼ teaspoon salt	1 pint milk

1 Sieve the flour and salt. Make a well in the centre and break the eggs into this.
2 Add about ¼ pint milk and stir, gradually working in the flour from the sides.
3 Add enough of the remaining milk to give a stiff batter consistency. Beat thoroughly for at least 5 minutes, then cover and leave to stand for 30 minutes.
4 Add remaining milk and stir well. Pour the mixture into a jug.

Flaky pastry

you will need:

8 oz. flour	squeeze lemon juice
pinch salt	cold water to mix
6 oz. equal quantities of	
margarine and lard	

1 Sieve flour and salt.
2 Cream fat until soft and pliable, and divide into 4 portions.
3 Rub one portion of fat into flour, add a squeeze lemon juice and sufficient cold water to make a soft dough.
4 Roll dough into an oblong. Cover two-thirds of the oblong with another portion of fat, dabbing it in small pieces over the dough.
5 Fold dough in three, starting at the bottom with the uncovered section. Bring this up to the centre of oblong. Bring the top third down over. Lightly press edges together with the rolling pin.
6 Half turn the pastry to the left and roll out into an oblong.
7 Repeat this process (5 and 6) twice, adding another portion of fat each time.
8 Fold the pastry in three once more, without adding fat.
9 Wrap in greaseproof paper or foil and leave in the refrigerator or a cold place for 1 hour before rolling out for use.

Note: If possible, leave the pastry to 'relax' in a cool place for about 10 minutes between each rolling.

Rough puff pastry

you will need:

8 oz. flour	1 teaspoon lemon juice
pinch salt	cold water to mix
6 oz. equal quantities of	
margarine and lard	

1 Sieve flour and salt.
2 Cut fat into small cubes, add to flour. Do not rub in.
3 Add lemon juice and sufficient cold water to mix to a fairly stiff dough.
4 Roll into an oblong, taking care not to stretch the pastry at the edges.
5 Fold pastry into three. Bring the bottom end two-thirds up and the top piece down to the folded edge.
6 Seal the edges by pressing lightly with a rolling pin.
7 Half turn the pastry to the left and roll it out into an oblong.
8 Repeat the process (5 and 6) twice.
9 Fold the pastry in three once more. Wrap it in greaseproof paper or foil and leave in a refrigerator or cold place for an hour before rolling out to use.

Note: This pastry is very similar to puff pastry but is easier and quicker to make. It can be used in any recipe that requires puff or flaky pastry.

Short crust pastry

you will need:

8 oz. flour	2 oz. lard (or vegetable
pinch salt	shortening)
2 oz. margarine	cold water to mix

1 Sieve flour and salt.
2 Roughly chop fat and add to flour. Rub fats into flour, using the finger tips, until mixture resembles breadcrumbs.
3 Gradually add cold water and knead mixture lightly by hand until it works together into a firm dough.
4 Turn on to a lightly floured surface and knead lightly until smooth. Turn pastry over and roll out as required.

Rich short crust or flan pastry

you will need:

8 oz. flour	1 egg yolk
pinch salt	1–2 tablespoons cold
5 oz. butter	water
1 teaspoon castor sugar	

1 Sieve flour and salt.
2 Rub butter lightly into the flour, using finger-tips, until mixture resembles fine breadcrumbs.
3 Add sugar and egg yolk, work into flour, add water gradually until mixture forms a firm dough.
4 Turn on to a floured surface, knead lightly and roll out.

Note: If the pastry is difficult to handle, leave in a cold place for at least 1 hour before using.

To make a flan case

cooking time: about 15 minutes

1. Make pastry as page 90.
2. Roll pastry into a circle about 2-inches larger than the flan ring.
3. Place flan ring on a baking sheet. Place the round of pastry over the ring and press into shape, taking care that the pastry fits well against the inside edge, but is not stretched.
4. Trim off surplus pastry by passing the rolling pin over the edge of the ring. Place a piece of lightly greased greaseproof paper, greased side down, in the flan and fill with uncooked rice, haricot beans or macaroni.
5. Bake in a moderately hot oven (400°F. – Gas Mark 6) for 15 minutes or until the pastry is firm.*
6. Remove filling and paper from flan. Return flan to oven for a further 5 minutes to allow base to cook through.
7. Remove flan ring and leave flan case on a wire tray until cold. Cold cooked pastry may be stored in an air-tight tin and used as required.

*Pastry baked in this way is described as 'baked blind'. This is done to ensure a good shape. The rice etc. can be stored in a jar and used indefinitely for this purpose.

Note: If the flan ring is not available, a sandwich tin may be used but, before the pastry is fitted, strips of strong paper should be placed across the inside of the tin to protrude at the edges. This will enable the flan case to be removed easily from the tin.

Suet pastry

you will need:

8 oz. self-raising flour (with plain flour, add 1 teaspoon baking powder)
pinch salt
4 oz. shredded suet
water to mix

1. Sieve flour and salt.
2. Add suet and mix in, using a long bladed-knife.
3. Stir in enough water to make a firm dough.
4. Knead lightly, roll out as required.

Tomato sauce

cooking time: about 30 minutes

you will need:

2 onions
2 tablespoons oil
1 small can tomato paste
pinch thyme
1 pint water
salt, pepper

1. Peel and chop the onions.
2. Heat the oil in a small pan and fry onions for about 5 minutes.
3. Add the tomato paste and cook for a few minutes longer, stirring all the time.
4. Add the thyme and water, boil gently for about 25 minutes. Season to taste.

Egg and butter sauce

cooking time: 5 minutes

you will need:

2 oz. unsalted butter
1 large hard-boiled egg
dash of Worcestershire sauce
1 teaspoon lemon juice
salt, pepper

1. Melt butter over gentle heat, do not allow to brown.
2. Shell egg and chop finely. Add to butter.
3. Add Worcestershire sauce, lemon juice and salt and pepper to taste. Serve sauce with cooked white fish or asparagus.

White sauce

cooking time: about 10 minutes

you will need:

1 oz. butter
1 oz. flour
½ pint milk
seasoning

1. Melt butter, stir in flour, using a wooden spoon.
2. Cook over a gentle heat for 3 minutes without browning, stirring throughout.
3. Remove from heat and gradually stir in half the milk, stir hard until well blended.
4. Return to heat, cook slowly until sauce thickens, stirring.
5. Gradually add remaining milk.
6. Bring to the boil, season with salt and pepper. Allow to boil for 2–3 minutes, stirring throughout. *This is a thick coating sauce,* used for cauliflower cheese, filling flans and baked casserole dishes.

For a thin or pouring sauce – use ½ oz. butter and ½ oz. flour. The amount of milk and method are the same.

Variations

Cheese sauce – to ½ pint white sauce add 2 heaped tablespoons grated cheese, a little made mustard, a little salt and a pinch Cayenne pepper. Add the cheese when the sauce is at boiling point, mix in well but do not allow the sauce to boil again.

Mushroom sauce – cook 2 oz. sliced mushrooms in ½ oz. butter very gently for about 5 minutes. Stir mushrooms, butter and juice from mushrooms into ½ pint hot white sauce. Season to taste.

Onion sauce – to ½ pint white sauce (made from ½ milk and ½ liquid in which the onions were cooked) add 2 chopped, boiled onions and a few drops of lemon juice.

Parsley sauce – to ½ pint boiling white sauce, add 1 heaped tablespoon chopped parsley and a squeeze lemon juice (optional).

Egg sauce – stir 1 or 2 chopped hard-boiled eggs into white sauce after it has boiled.

Sweet sauce – omit seasoning, stir 1 oz. sugar and 2 or 3 drops of flavouring essence into ½ pint hot white sauce. Stir until sugar is dissolved.

Index

92